Contents

Challenging
the More Able
Language User

Geoff Dean

David Fulton Publishers

London

in association with

The National Association for Able Children in Education

David Fulton Publishers Ltd
Ormond House, 26–27 Boswell Street, London WC1N 3JD

First published in Great Britain by David Fulton Publishers 1998

British Library Cataloguing in Publication Data
A catalogue record for this book is available from the British Library

ISBN 1–85346–517–8

Typeset by FSH Print & Production Ltd.
Printed in Great Britain by The Cromwell Press Ltd, Trowbridge, Wilts.

With love and thanks to my family:
Bryony, my muse, and Karen and Jack
for their patience, help and support

Preface

'I'm sorry that your daughter can read, she will miss so much.'
Headteacher of infant school to mother of incoming child.

This is a true story. A little girl born into a language-rich, middle class home shows an early aptitude for words. She chatters intelligently as a toddler and at two and a half years is beginning to read by decoding letters and using her prodigious visual memory. After another year or so, the little girl makes discernible marks on paper, indicating she has reached the early stages of identifiable writing; her own name and members of the family ('mummy', 'daddy','granny' etc.) her first successes.

A few weeks before her fourth birthday the girl begins her formal education in a local nursery school. At the parents' evening some months later, a kindly and committed teacher, whom the child adores, leans over to the parents and shares the following information, whispered almost like a secret: 'We know ..... can read and write, but we don't do anything about it.' The parents are a little surprised.

Before the little girl becomes a pupil at her infant school, a year later, the parents supply detailed information to the headteacher about her reading fluency and her ability as a writer. She already makes informed choices of books from the local library, selecting stories by author and theme. She reads at every possible opportunity and retells stories vividly. Despite this preparation, the reception class teacher still shows surprise when she discovers, on the child's first day, that the girl can read. Having no other strategies prepared, the teacher sends the child to a classroom for older children to borrow one of their books, *The Battle of Bubble and Squeak*, which she reads easily, for the time being.

The parents approach the school regularly to ask for extra support for the child, and even suggest a few activities which might challenge her, within the context of her other work alongside the pupils in her class. Nothing out of the ordinary, however, is supplied, and the parents are made to feel as if they are a nuisance! The child continues to borrow a selection of 'older' books, which she consumes at a rapid rate on a nightly basis. At home, the parents are keen to see what the child is capable of, and, wrapping them as far as possible in normal domestic discussion and play, suggest a few activities which she might enjoy attempting. These include written arguments (one about Brazilian rain forests, then an interest) and, with her very young brother, devising a short radio play using some monster and spaceship sound effects! She copes with both admirably. Becoming interested in animation, she uses the pause facility on a video camera to make some short films, featuring adventures of her Playmobil toy characters. She chooses suitable music and writes scripts for post-production overdubs. All whilst still in Key Stage 1.

During the next few years the school continues to miss many opportunities to provide extension tasks, although the girl explores a wide range of language forms at home. She writes about the violin, which she has begun to play, after researching the topic; as a result of a canal holiday, she composes a sustained first person narrative of narrow boat life a century ago, after more research; becoming skilled in word-processing, she writes a review of a theatre trip in a newspaper style, having studied newspaper reviews of the same production; enjoying two Jane Austen novels, she writes a semi-critical essay about 'the world as it appears in Austen's works'. This latter at about the same time as her headteacher dissuades her from reading *Jane Eyre* at school ('too difficult') and sends her home with a copy of *The Borrowers* instead. She drafts all her work, often discarding two or three versions before arriving at, what she believes to be, the final finished piece. Poetry, correspondence with adults, diaries of holidays are further examples of different text types with which she becomes familiar and enjoys writing.

Hoping that her secondary school will properly recognise her linguistic abilities and make the most of them, the girl's parents put together an extensive folder of samples of her work, including the detailed book list of her reading over a period of three years. These are sent to the receiving Head of English in anticipation of an improved working relationship. The parents receive no reply, and it is evident that the school makes no extra arrangements, beyond an occasional general language session with a special needs teacher, in the company of two other able pupils. The child embarks on mainstream English lessons, writing a detailed autobiography, carefully structured and drafted, as one of her tasks. Yet little other practice of text types is expected, and she is not challenged by any target-setting, which might increase her accomplishment. She enjoys and is stimulated by an after-school writing club, supervised by a member of the English department. Yet her writing is not monitored by any member of staff, no discussions take place with the girl about the enormous range of texts she is daily encountering. She is a prize winner in a national writing competition.

In Year 8 the English programme becomes so slow and protracted – a straightforward novel shared by the whole class takes almost a term to study – the child grows increasingly frustrated and bored. English as a school subject becomes the child's least favourite lesson. Asked yet again to meet the girl's needs, the school is unable to offer more than the occasional conversation with the Head of the English department. She is a prize winner in the same national writing competition a year later.

During the year of her Key Stage 3 SAT test her class studies *Romeo and Juliet*.

Having seen the play performed by the RSC at The Barbican, watched Zeffirelli's production on video – from choice – three times, been enthralled with Luhrmann's new film version and read the play through with her brother and father, she has considerable knowledge of and insight into the play. Yet no provision is made for the girl to work on the text in a way which would more appropriately reflect her head start. Just as no particularly special programme of tasks has been made available for the previous nine years of formal education within the school context.

This girl's story is not so very unusual. It might be familiar to a great many parents. When I first began talking about this topic to teachers, a few in the audience regularly told me that they too had encountered similar disappointments and frustrations in respect of their own children, mostly girls. The main character of this narrative is not a 'genius', nor some sort of child prodigy. Her linguistic talents have advantaged the way she makes better sense of the rest of the curriculum, certainly, but she would not qualify as 'gifted' on most criteria; she is more able. Yet she has not herself made a fuss or any special demands on the school. She joins in with the activities in her classroom, mostly with enthusiasm, and regularly produces impressive and accurate work, usually more than the expected minimum and occasionally exceptional because of genuine interest. But she is aware that insufficient demands are being made on her and that there are alternative ways of exploring the textual problems she has encountered. She knows that there is more meaning to be found in the books which have been put in front of her, although these approaches are not hinted at or taught.

I am not suggesting that the teachers who worked with this child deliberately delayed her progress or intended to make her tread water academically. I am claiming that most of them really did not know what to do about the situation they faced. All of them commented at different times on the girl's significant ability, but they had no means of using it as a starting point for further development. What was fortunate about this particular case was the continued commitment the child had to her reading and writing, outside school. Other children also continue with their interest in linguistic activities, though not at a level they might be achieving; a few, mostly boys, lose their motivation, become bored and – not unusually – disaffected.

Pupils of this calibre can be difficult to identify. Most do not make a fuss about their interest in books at an early stage and quietly continue to participate through ordinary ways in the expected activities of their classrooms, without drawing attention to themselves. Their writing is likely to indicate their emerging potential, but their teachers are often pleased with the results of the child's written tasks, without building on them in a way which could accelerate development. There are also other pressures on children to prevent them from making a claim on extra teacher time, including the sense of many young people that to show off special talents is unacceptable. There is a distinct 'anti-boff' (from the idea of 'boffin', or clever scientist) culture in many schools from the earliest years. It is not cool to be clever! Many boys are sensitive to this form of labelling and would rather remain anonymous than indicate that they have special talents. Researchers Molly Warrington and Mike Younger, from Homerton College, Cambridge, quoted in the *TES*, discovered that many boys thought it was not acceptable for them to appear to be interested in or stimulated by academic work. Many secondary pupils are reluctant to be seen in this role, and they are just as likely to be the able pupils as the more average ones.

Yet there are also considerable numbers of parents who have prepared their children in different ways, with more or less intent, for the rigours of school, through what Shirley Brice Heath calls their 'literacy events', who are disappointed by the sluggish or non-existent reactions of teachers to their children's already developed skills in the early years. They feel frustrated about the apparent lack of challenge their children are given, they believe that the reading demands are undeveloped and have a sense that the low expectations of the teachers fail to stretch their children's intellects. Indeed, a sizable proportion of middle class parents make an early decision about their children not participating in state education because they believe that their children will not be given opportunities to take full advantage of their precocious attainment.

This book is intended to help teachers and schools prepare for children who display talents beyond the ordinary in reading and writing, and usually speaking. It will contain suggested ways of identifying pupils who show these skills and recommend methods of assessing them which could prompt teachers to think about 'what next?' in regard to their developing accomplishments. 'What next?' is one of the most important phrases in the whole book! There will be recommendations about the possible approaches to language and literacy growth which will best accommodate and challenge able language users. I have listed a sample of activities likely to engage them fully, with real interest, many already tried out with appropriate pupils in real classroom settings, but some offered as natural extension ventures.

Part of the purpose of this work is to allow schools to celebrate the fact that there are children with special abilities on the roll, who should be viewed with pride. In a time when schools must regard themselves as increasingly accountable, it is essential that they have ways of recognising that there are pupils with pronounced skills, who are being properly catered for and who are achieving their full capabilities. To miss these children, or to fail to provide the sorts of challenge to which they will respond and grow, is to fail the pupils, the parents and the community as a whole.

Just as important, however, is every school's obligation to provide for the capabilities of all pupils. It is my claim that if the school is giving proper consideration to its more able language users, and drawing from them the best they can attain, it will be doing the same for all the rest of its pupils. To raise expectations for one group should have beneficial results for the other groups in the school, because staff will be thinking more carefully about what the implications of teaching and learning in language mean for all the children. Those expectations, however, will never be high enough unless the teachers have a guiding vision about what the purposes of language, literacy and literary studies should be in their own school. Only by articulating and sharing a clear sense of the way in which children grow and progress linguistically, and of what they might be capable of achieving, can the primary school or English department be confident of evincing the best from its pupils.

A further consideration which should convince schools of the importance of proper provision for pupils identified as more able language users is that by paying the fullest attention to linguistic skills, the broader learning abilities of the pupils concerned will also be enhanced. The Russian psychologist, Vygotsky, writing in the 1930s, pointed to the complex interaction between language and the development of knowledge as:

..... a continual movement back and forth from thought to word and from word to thought. In that process, the relation of thought to word undergoes changes ..... thought is not merely expressed in words; it comes into existence through them. Every thought tends to connect something with something else, to establish a relation between them. Every thought moves, grows and develops, fulfils a function, solves a problem. (Vygotsky, 1986)

The dynamic and interactive relationship between the development of concepts and language means that thoughts prompt language, which – through speaking, or writing or reading – will, in turn, bring about further thinking. Language and thought can be seen as inextricably linked in this association. To develop the language potential of the more able is also to develop the learning and thinking capacities they will employ in all areas of their education.

'Able' or 'more able' are difficult qualities to define in relation to language. The assessment of English and English language use has caused enormous argument over the past few decades and has been the topic of most dispute in many English departments in secondary schools since the introduction of the National Curriculum. The original 10-level scale imposed to assess English attainment was not a structure securely based on the ways children learn and acquire language. Brian Cox, the Chair of the English group which recommended the first National Curriculum Orders, does not explore the problems his committee faced when expected to make sense of the injunction in his record of their deliberations:

..... ten different levels of attainment should be identified within each target covering all the years of compulsory schooling. *Pupils' progress should be registered against these levels* [my italics]: level 2 *should be assumed to represent the performance of the median 7 year old* [my italics]. (Cox, 1991)

It was a difficult enough structure for teachers to use in their attempts to make overall assessments of their pupils' English abilities, based on all the language interactions in which they saw them engaged. The eight-level scale which arbitrarily replaced the original system during a period of National Curriculum reform only confused matters further. But there is more to the whole assessment apparatus than the teachers' view: all pupils also have to participate in tests which focus on tiny portions of the whole English and language curriculum for closer scrutiny. Interpreting those criteria for the purposes of awarding overall levels at Key Stage 3, particularly, has still not been resolved five years after the introduction of the process.

The sorts of pupils covered by this book are not intended to be identified by the Level scales described above, and no number is intended to be attached to them. They are likely to be displaying skills and understanding in advance of their peers across a range of language activities which are evident enough without having to apply a test of any description. The ways in which they ought to be identified are explored in more detail in a later chapter.

It has not been usual to find English departments which have regularly sought more able language users, and planned a suitable programme of extension for them. My explanation for this state of affairs is given in greater detail in Chapter 1, but some recent historical background might be useful in understanding why certain attitudes and practices have become common in large numbers of secondary schools.

When Cox stepped warily into the English subject battlefield in the late 1980s with the first subject-based National Curriculum recommendations, he was quickly made aware of the tremendous diversity of approaches different departments felt towards the subject.

> It is possible to identify within the English teaching profession a number of different views of the subject. We list them here, though we stress that they are not the only possible views, they are not sharply distinguishable, and they are certainly not mutually exclusive. (DES, 1989)

As a means of drawing these opinions together for the purposes of worthwhile debate, he found it necessary to represent the ways in which approaches to the subject are perceived through five different 'models': personal growth, cultural heritage, cultural analysis, adult needs and cross-curricular.

While these categories are not much more than caricatures, having some insight into them does help to explain why less attention had been paid to articulating ideas of language/literacy progression during the previous twenty years than might have been expected. The Cox Committee set them out in this form:

a) a 'personal growth' view focuses on the child: it emphasises the relationships between language and learning in the individual child, and the role of literature in developing children's imaginative and aesthetic lives;

b) a 'cross-curricular' view focuses on the school: it emphasises that all teachers (of English and other subjects) have a responsibility to help children with the language demands of different subjects on the school curriculum: otherwise areas of the curriculum may be closed to them. In England, English is different from the other school subjects in that it is both a subject and medium of instruction for other subjects;

c) an 'adult needs' view focuses on communication outside the school: it emphasises the responsibility of English teachers to prepare children for the language demands of adult life, including the workplace, in a fast changing world. Children need to learn to deal with the day-to-day demands of spoken language and of print: they also need to be able to write clearly, appropriately and effectively;

d) a 'cultural heritage' view emphasises the responsibility of schools to lead children to an appreciation of those works of literature that have been widely regarded as amongst the finest in the language;

e) a 'cultural analysis' view emphasises the role of English in helping children towards a critical understanding of the world and cultural environment in which they live. Children should know about the processes by which meanings are conveyed, and about the ways in which print and other media carry values. (DES, 1989)

These models were proposed in a climate where it was perceived that there was no sole, clearly understood approach to the subject by the majority of English departments. It was, however, believed that most English teachers were guided by a mixture of all these views, but in differing proportions, in their approach to the way they regarded, planned and taught the subject. Andy Goodwyn, in research undertaken soon after these terms were first employed, discovered from the sample of English teachers he questioned that:

Cox's five models are recognised by a wide range of English teachers and his claim that they are generally present in English departments seems to be true, although there is evidence to suggest that the cross-curricular is not an English teacher's model ..... English teachers do have varying priorities for four of these models. ..... The survey confirms the personal growth model developed in the 1960s and 1970s remains dominant. (Goodwyn, 1992)

I would like to suggest that, partly because of political pressures and partly because of changing and evolving perspectives adopted in regard to knowledge and understanding of texts generally, if the poll was to be repeated today there would be a different result. The 'personal view' model has not been discredited, but the pressing relevance of 'cultural analysis' and the increasing insistence of the 'cross-curricular' models have had a strong effect on the ways teachers of English have come to see their work. The injunction on English teachers to be more precise about describing stages of progression in their subject, particularly in relation to their pupils' abilities in reading and writing of texts, has also pointed to a shift in ways of working. These changes should generally be welcomed, and they have certainly given a new focus to considerations which are likely to benefit more able language users. The trends that I have traced in the subject, in the briefest of detail, are intended to show that the context in which more able pupils can now be recognised and catered for has become more secure and relevant.

The National Association for Able Children in Education
Westminster College, Oxford OX2 9AT

The Association that Helps Teachers Help Able and Talented Children

AIMS

- To raise awareness of the particular educational needs which able and talented children have, in order to realise their full potential.

- To be proactive in promoting discussion and debate by raising relevant issues through liasion with educational policy makers.

- To ensure a broad, balanced and appropriate curriculum for able and talented children.

- To advocate the use of a differentiated educational provision in the classroom through curriculum enrichment and extension.

- To encourage commitment to the personal, social and intellectual development of the whole child.

- To make education an enjoyable, exciting and worthwhile experience for the able and talented.

Acknowledgements

This book has been a long time in preparation and has grown naturally from a great many encounters with others who have a similar interest in language and the way young people grow in their knowledge, understanding and love of language.

I owe more than I can ever properly express to Sylvia Karavis, Jenny Monk, Pat Davies, Jean Lowery, Paula Iley, Julie Daw and Hilda Read, all members of the Oxfordshire Primary Advisory Group in English (PAGE) at various times during the years I worked in the county. Their experience, enthusiasm and ability were widely recognised, and they actually made a positive difference to the practice of hundreds of teachers. I have also been grateful for the help and interest of Deborah Eyre, who has allowed me to share ideas about able language users, and encouraged my wider research, considerably adding to my knowledge of this topic.

My thanks are also extended to the Heads of English departments in Oxfordshire during the 1990s, who have allowed me to work alongside them, learning from their practice, and who have sometimes tested my ideas. Their continued loyalty and considerable contributions in meetings and personal discussions have shaped so much of what I have recently learned.

I wish, also, to express my thanks to the young people, many attending schools in Oxfordshire, who have shared material with me, let me see their writing and discussed their reading. I have been constantly excited about their ability and the quality of their work. I have been pleased to use poems and writing from St Philip and St James First School, Oxford; Great Tew Primary School; St Andrew's CE Primary School, Chinnor; Isis CE Middle School, Oxford; and St Birinus Primary School, Dorchester. Being able to see the 'extension' reading at St Mary's RC School, Bicester, was also a real pleasure. Finally, particular thanks to Catherine and her family for their enormous help.

The author wishes to thank the publishers and editors for permission to reprint extracts from the following copyright material:

Cairney, T. *Teaching Reading Comprehension* (1990) Open University Press. Chambers, A. *Booktalk* (1985) Thimble Press. Cox, B. *Cox on Cox* (1991) Hodder & Stoughton. Davies, C. *What is English Teaching?* (1996) Open University Press. Goodwyn, A. 'English teachers and the Cox Models' *English in Education*, NATE, Autumn 1992 **26**(3). Hayhoe, M. and Parker, S. *Working with Fiction* (1984) Arnold. Lewis, M. and Wray, D. *Developing Children's Non-fiction Writing* (1995) Scholastic. Littlefair, A. *Reading All Types of Writing* (1990) Open University Press. Monk, J. and Karavis, S. 'Developing the reading of non-fiction' in *Reading On!* Reid, D. and Bentley, D. (eds) (1996) Scholastic. Monk, J. 'The language of argument in the writing of young children' in *Looking into Language* Bain, R., Fitzgerald B., and Taylor, M. (eds) (1992) Hodder & Stoughton. Peim, N. 'Key Stage 4: Back to the Future' in *The Challenge of English in the National Curriculum* Protherough, R and King, P. (eds) (1995) Routledge. Styles, M., and Drummond, M. J., (eds) *The Politics of Reading* University of Cambridge, Institute of Education, Homerton College, Cambridge. Vygotsky, L. *Thought and Language* ed. Alex Kozulin (1986) The Massachusetts Institute of Technology. Webster, A., Beveridge, M., and Reed, M. *Managing the Literacy Curriculum* (1996) Routledge. Wray, D., and Lewis, M. *Extending Literacy: Children Reading and Writing Non-fiction* (1997) Routledge.

Chapter 1

The Problem

'Your son is a Level 4 reader,' the delighted teacher informed the parent of a Year 2 child.
'That's good news,' the parent replied, 'what is the school doing about it?'

In 1997 Deborah Eyre, President of the National Association for Able Children in Education (NACE), published a book, *Able Children in Ordinary Schools*, in which she indicated an increasing awareness in schools of the numbers of pupils they admit who have 'significant ability' in particular areas of the school curriculum. Until quite recently, she asserts, schools tended to recognise their 'more able' pupils only if they displayed all-round or overall abilities, which usually meant that very few children were selected for special attention. Changing the ways of interpreting assessment data to identify those who show notable ability in, for instance, history or science, but not necessarily both, indicated to some schools that there are many more pupils who would benefit from provision which meets their needs more precisely. 'A focus on specific ability as well as all-round ability helps to maximise pupil potential and has the added advantage of helping to raise school standards and examination results.' (Eyre, 1997)

Children who show early notable performance in mathematics or music often enjoy enhanced support for their talents, through activities organised inside school and beyond. Those who display sporting ability when very young are usually able to join suitable clubs and are often encouraged to participate in coaching courses, to increase their skills. Unfortunately, for a number of reasons, similar identification of pupils who are able users of language has not been as regularly undertaken and the children who might be regarded as fitting this description have not been developed in the possible ways their early potential should have suggested.

The earliest stages of schooling

A large number of children enter infant education each year already able to read and making marks on paper which are recognisably the beginnings of writing. The majority of these pupils are not infant prodigies; they come from homes no longer fearful of the reproving eye of the receiving reception class teacher, who once believed it was the school's exclusive province to teach reading. (The quotation at the beginning of the Preface is absolutely true, and utterly typical of an attitude which prevailed in infant schools for many years.) These children bring into school the rich totality of their 'literacy events', as Shirley Brice Heath calls the story telling and other wealth of language interactions these children have encountered with adults, other children and the wider world. Many other young pupils are on the verge of a breakthrough to reading and writing, merely requiring help of a focused kind to make the progress of which they are capable. Far too few are given the extra support or special provision likely to enhance their already developing abilities, and nothing in the school documentation recognises their presence or suggests the measures they may require, beyond those offered to all mainstream pupils.

The evidence continues to grow from large numbers of OFSTED reports from inspections of both primary and secondary schools, in all parts of the country, containing specific recommendations to 'challenge' or 'make proper provision for the more able' in English and language activities. This is a national problem. My own observations, made during the course of many OFSTED inspections and curriculum monitoring visits as an LEA inspector, sitting in hundreds of lessons, also confirms that too many able language users fail to be recognised properly in their schools. Or, where they are known, they are too often not fully motivated, challenged or engaged.

The pupils to whom these recommendations refer are either regarded as a convenience, seemingly needing less direct attention than their more average classmates, affording a little extra time for their teachers; or they are 'invisible', with their teachers failing to notice their attributes, treating them in the same manner as the rest of the class. Schools regularly pride themselves on making proper provision for those who, for a variety of reasons, fall behind with literacy skills, yet many do not pay sufficient attention to the equally important needs of those who are already well 'above average' on arrival.

This situation is partly understandable, for the following reasons. Teachers of the youngest children usually have to deal with large classes, working hard to implement a proper literacy curriculum for the greatest number of pupils possible, in a short time. Some teachers, particularly those in classrooms in difficult areas of social deprivation, work against enormous odds. In these circumstances, it is reasonable to see why they plan a blanket programme of language and literacy study for the mainstream children, with extra support for those who are already identified as lagging behind their peers. The assessment procedures at the end of Key Stage 1 only require the teacher to bring as many pupils as possible to an understood 'normal' standard, with no extra reward afforded to the classroom which exceeds this level. There is little incentive to encourage pupils to move 'further into reading', or to explore the wider implications of improved writing ability, once these basic skills have been put to use in the child's learning apparatus.

At this, the earliest stage of education, teachers are not looking out for specific subject-related ability, so the assessment repertoire they employ does not readily point out those who are displaying unusually good attainment.

The junior years

At Key Stage 2, primary teachers have to take responsibility for introducing increasing amounts of work across a wide range of subjects, to meet the demands of the National Curriculum, with the result that the English/language/literacy curriculum moves gradually into the background.

> Literacy (and numeracy) become the **contexts for learning**. What used to be the object of schooling becomes (slowly) the normal daily routine. Children are expected and required to **know how**: how to read this; how to write that; how to manage this event in which literacy is situated; how to choose this convention and not that convention. (Reed, 1996)

While pupils who read confidently across a range of texts and who write more fluently in a variety of forms are advantaged in general terms across the curriculum, too little opportunity is afforded to increasing the attainment in those linguistic areas in which they have shown extra talent. The actual *teaching* of reading, these days more clearly and confidently articulated by teachers of pupils in Key Stage 1, is much less securely understood or practised in Key Stage 2. This situation often means that pupils' skills, awoken and activated with real vigour, are not fully consolidated at this later stage.

A NATE paper of the late 1980s (Barrett, P. *et al.*, 'Learning to be Literate in a Democratic Society') captures this shortfall precisely, quoting evidence from the National Assessment Education Progress:

> By yesterday's standards the news is good: 95% can read and understand the printed word.
>
> In terms of tomorrow's needs, there is cause for concern: only a small percentage can understand complex material.

Much of the writing expected of children during this Key Stage is of a limited, commonplace nature, mainly reporting on work or topics completed, or consisting of undifferentiated narrative, of itself not requiring much actual teaching. In this climate, pupils who write effortlessly make some progress, but much less than they might if proper levels of expectation had been established and planned for.

The notion of English/language 'progression' in junior schools is not often confidently shared by the staff or described in their documentation. It is not unusual to find some children in the school being asked to take part in very similar linguistic activities in all the different year groups of the school, without any properly planned criteria for growth. So pupils in Year 3 might be asked to write letters, like their school companions in Year 6, with no discernible difference in the outcomes, or no particular extra qualities being sought by the older pupils. In the same setting it is not unusual to find the assessment of reading leading to the encouragement of tackling superficially 'harder' books, without in any way probing the breadth and range of analytical skills the pupil could be mastering. It is quite possible to be talented in language-based activities in such an environment and yet take no real steps forward, simply because the teachers do not know how to plan work at the level the child can achieve.

Junior to secondary school

Standard assessment tests (SATs) administered at the end of Key Stage 2, when most pupils transfer from primary to secondary schools, have begun to establish a standard of achievement expected of pupils at the age of 11. Yet the English tests are not carefully focused and fail to asses the ability of pupils across a range of language usage. There is also evidence that secondary schools have not yet begun to recognise this testing procedure as a worthwhile indicator of how prepared pupils will be to meet the more demanding requirements of the secondary curriculum, and they disregard the results. Secondary English teachers are also aware that the awarding of a Level 5 in the subject at the end of Key Stage 2 currently has no standardised relationship with the awarding of a Level 5 at the end of Key Stage 3, some three years of schooling later. This problem is being investigated by the assessment authorities. As a consequence of these anomalies and lack of confidence in the test results, cohorts of pupils continue to move to the senior school and 'begin again', without enjoying the chance to build on their current attainment. Because many of these youngsters are then placed in mixed ability English groups for the first year or first two years of their secondary careers, where 'differentiation' is not always fully understood, the able language users can be easily missed, and not have appropriately challenging tasks designed for them.

With the best of intentions, and in line with a particular 'model' of the subject they have most frequently espoused – the 'personal growth' view, described in the Preface – English teachers supporting and encouraging Key Stage 3 pupils have believed in:

> ... an essentially non-competitive, non-hierarchical approach to the subject. It is not concerned with linear progression but much more with a widening spiral notion of the development in which the individual steadily improves over the four language modes but within that improvement there is a constant recursion and stimulation of various kinds, including teaching which may lead to sudden spurts of growth. (Goodwyn, 1995)

Chris Davies, in *What is English Teaching?*, makes a slightly different but related claim when he writes:

> English teachers have often tended to be quite unfocused in the way they define their aims. That is to say, they often view what goes on in their classrooms in a very inclusive way, so that everything that happens in a lesson is counted as contributing to students' learning ...
>
> All this seems fair enough, and in some ways desirable, but if learning is in

everything then it might sometimes be difficult to know whether or not it happened. (Davies, 1996)

If there are questions to be raised about the actual lack of focus on learning resulting from this approach, and I think there are, I would like to suggest that more able pupils suffer proportionally more than other pupils. These particular young people are capable of looking more precisely at the nature of their work, by definition, and yet they are being denied those precise grounds of learning on which to base their judgments about themselves.

Teachers of English regularly use the phrase 'differentiation by outcome', when planning and setting work for pupils in Years 7 to 9, with the implied suggestion that the more able will drift up to the surface. There they will be easily recognisable by their (usually written) work of significantly greater quality, and, on occasions, quantity. What this approach fails to distinguish is that the more able are probably capable of outcomes or results in excess of those they are currently achieving, even when their achievement is already greater than that of their classmates. If the potential extent of these possible 'outcomes' has not been properly explored at the planning stage, who can ascertain whether they have been realised? Teacher and pupil really should be sharing a view of what is possible, if the genuinely possible is to reached. A colleague adviser once suggested that 'differentiation by outcome' could just as well be applied to classroom settings where a teacher is not present!

Another shortcoming of the 'differentiation by outcome' approach is when pupils sense that those outcomes (usually written) are regarded as final products, rather than being thought of as achievements at particular points along a developmental process. One way to avoid this misunderstanding is to encourage the view that all written work is in 'draft' form; the final, published version has merely been an arbitrarily chosen moment at which further reconsideration has been ended. Given more time, it would have been possible to have continued the task.

Some English teachers have been reluctant to nominate pupils as 'more able' in the past. They have been aware that a few pupils display extra linguistics qualities which they enjoy seeing, but they have made no particular arrangements to support such pupils which might identify them as more talented in their classroom. On the one hand, it could be that these teachers are unhappy to establish what they, mistakenly, think of as a 'sheep and goats' situation, where to pick out a small group of pupils for special attention would be thought of as elitist. This attitude, I contend, actually disadvantages every member of the school. The more able lose ground, because they are not being required to work at levels commensurate with their ability, and the other pupils could be working at a more elevated level, in the 'slipstream' of the most talented. Far from unfairly favouring a small group of able pupils, their deliberate recognition is an important step in the process of raising expectations about what the standards of achievement could mean across the whole department. On the other hand, this reluctance might have been as a result of teachers' uncertainty with assessment procedures:

... teachers of English ... are working with a composite model made up from a complex interrelationship between four important models of English. As Personal Growth colours everything they do, so it becomes essential to view ability in the subject as a complex, dynamic element, more of a process than a simple observable product. (Goodwyn, 1995)

Where pupils' linguistic abilities *are* recognised, especially those of more able readers, the strategies employed to develop and encourage their skills have been, in my experience, limited. More able girl readers, particularly, are often introduced to a 'classical' literary heritage, and have texts such as *Jane Eyre*, *Wuthering Heights* and *Pride and Prejudice* placed in their hands, if they have not already discovered them for themselves. It is as if significant reading ability requires a diet of texts written before 1900 to keep it alive and thriving! Teachers who have favourably subscribed to a 'personal growth' model of English for the majority of their pupils, in most circumstances, appear to switch effortlessly to a 'cultural heritage' view when confronted with the challenge of the more able. This remedy, interestingly, is not generally applied to boys with any great success. Yet pupils of both genders are not usually directed towards a broad repertoire of more modern texts, which might interest and engage them. Nor are they encouraged to reflect on their current and past reading practices, likes and dislikes, with any view to discovering the sorts of texts which might be suitable to support their future reading growth, which I suggest are just as important.

Like their younger counterparts in the primary school, these adolescent pupils are more likely to be challenged by their teachers through a perceived increasing 'difficulty' of text, when they could, just as effectively, be taking advantage of a programme designed to broaden their experiences in a comparative study of contemporary works, written for their age group. Caroline St John Brooks' research into the nature of English departments in the 1980s, quoted by Chris Davies, revealed this attitude of English staff, who:

... whilst not denying the importance of literacy skills, consider them as a means to an end, the end being a fuller and freer, more critical and more constructive inner life for their students. This, they believe, can best be achieved in dialogue with the minds of others, through the medium of literature. (Davies, 1996)

Interestingly, Brooks detected that some English departments, as a result of this commitment to transmitting and sharing the best of the literary canon, found it difficult not to favour more academic children who could make greater sense of their reading. This attitude is illustrated in an extract from one department's policy documentation: 'As a department we feel that there are some well-known works and types of literature with which at least the more able of our pupils should, at some stage, become acquainted.' (Quoted in Davies, 1996). This statement at least recognises that there could be a possibility that more able pupils might be dealing with a more demanding reading diet than is to be found in the mainstream English curriculum, even if the only hesitant provision to be suggested is the exploration of one rather limited area of literary study.

Unlike younger more able pupils, those in secondary school find it harder to maintain their enthusiasm for independent study or work in English, although quite a few continue to read, voraciously and surreptitiously, texts which they know will not necessarily be endorsed by their schools. Whereas younger children are often happy to write poetry or stories beyond the normal expectations of their lessons because they enjoy the activity, more mature pupils lose that motivation unless an informed adult shows some sensitive interest in their efforts and offers direction or advice about their output. This development is also one which is not easy to supervise without proper preparation. Teachers – in all phases – often find it difficult to assess the creative work of their pupils. They sometimes feel unable to suggest areas of improvement, believing that to meddle in their pupils' work is to destroy the spirit in which it was conceived. Poetry holds special fears for many teachers, who then fail to urge the best results from their pupils, worried that young writers will be hurt by criticism, when it should be supporting the search for clearer and stronger meaning.

Older pupils also have many other attractions and distractions to occupy them, not least the demanding rigours of the rest of the school curriculum. Unless they are engaged at the level of personal and genuine interest, they have little reason to continue with these literary occupations and the areas of potential they once began to exhibit are likely to wither.

Older pupils

As they arrive in Key Stage 4, aged 14, pupils embark on their GCSE courses. Nearly all English departments place their pupils in ability sets at this point in the school and the more able language pupils are usually placed in the higher ability sets. Their rate of progress will often increase at this time because the level of study demanded of their examination texts is more suitably planned. A few show an aptitude for wider study abilities, related to their curriculum, and teachers reward and support their efforts. Yet most could have been making greater progress from an earlier stage in their schooling, enabling them to participate in a much more demanding, and ultimately more satisfying, programme of literary analysis, enhancing their own opportunities and those of their classmates.

For a few, the restricted diet of reading and writing continues until the end of Year 11, with the department failing to encourage the fullest familiarisation of a broad and exciting canon, even though the pupils might achieve excellent grades in the final examination. There are some pupils at this stage who, having been identified by the English department as more able, are placed in the 'fast track', meaning that they might be placed in an accelerated programme whereby they are entered for GCSE a year, or in rare cases, two years earlier than their chronological age. Despite this extra attention, however, there are instances where inadequate follow-up after the examination has meant that pupils lose the advantage from which they initially benefited.

The preparation of such pupils for their A level studies is too regularly undeveloped. In the sixth form the literary programme suddenly becomes more difficult through the types of analytical questions being asked of texts and the necessity of drawing on a wider variety of texts becomes a prerequisite, yet the most able students have not been rehearsed in practising these techniques. They almost have to 'relearn' an approach to texts, which is wasteful of their own time and prevents these students from offering the sort of academic example to others which could make their courses proceed with real gusto.

Other problems

Primary and secondary schools do not usually make the best sort of provision for pupils with more advanced linguistic and language abilities, because they are not looking out for them. They do not anticipate their arrival and do not notice their presence. Many schools also fail to have in place the necessary language-enhancing curriculum which would allow these pupils to thrive. The curriculum for English is, undoubtedly, one of the most difficult for primary schools to plan and implement. Unless there is somebody on the staff who has an academic background in the subject, or who has attended worthwhile INSET, there is often little real guidance of teaching and learning to bring about significant language and literacy growth. I am still asked by teachers who have been designated the post of 'language coordinator' in a primary school if there is a useful Scheme of Work already published which they could adopt for their school, or, even worse, 'is there a good text book?' Teachers cannot be blamed for this situation; they have to accommodate and implement a ten subject curriculum in the primary years. They do not have the luxury of giving too great a priority to one subject area, such as English, important as it may be in supporting greater attainment for the majority of pupils in all their other subjects.

The teaching of reading has improved enormously at Key Stage 1, and many more teachers are able to articulate their strategies for helping pupils to understand and grow with the texts they encounter. It is also more usual to hear teachers of initial reading talk about a wider range of approaches, where there once tended to be a stronger affinity to a single methodology. Yet there are still too few really comprehensive schemes for assessing reading in place. The school is pleased when pupils are seen to be dealing with texts independently, without promulgating further ways in which pupils might be helped to develop reading skills. Similarly, when writers are regarded as operating most successfully by themselves, without requiring too much extra support, they are perceived as having attained a particularly important goal in its own right, requiring no additional stages. Further demands, through familiarisation with a greater range of types of texts, are not then made. While reading and writing are always regarded as essential skills, and schools do their best to help pupils achieve well in them, significantly more searching questions such as 'reading for which purposes?' or 'what is the range of reading we should be covering?' are not asked by teachers often enough. The failure to ask similar questions, such as 'what is the purpose of this writing?', 'how do pupils learn about writing, and learn in the contexts which has brought about the writing?' and 'what is the possible range of writing we should be teaching?', results in full achievement being forestalled for many pupils.

In Key Stage 2 classes of many primary schools, and in the majority of secondary schools, there is little evidence to indicate that the notion of 'teaching of reading' is well understood. Most of the pupils can already read, teachers have claimed in the past, and why should staff spend valuable time on that task when there is so much else to get through? This situation usually results from a misunderstanding about the potential scope of 'reading', which does not look far beyond straightforward decoding skills, which will enable pupils to practise limited 'comprehension' exercises.

> While our understanding of the reading process has increased in the last 20 years, few changes seem to have occurred in the way comprehension has been taught. A generation of teachers has had the opportunity to share in the results of research which has shown that reading is a constructive process driven by the search for meaning, and yet most still teach comprehension as if it were simply a process of information transfer. Passages are set and questions designed to interrogate them. Little concern is shown for the reader, and the knowledge he or she brings to the text is largely ignored. Comprehension is taught as a skills-based process that can be separated from the readings of real-world texts for functional purposes. (Cairney, 1990)

If teachers of English have been slow to change their teaching of 'reading' to seek the fullest meaning, their colleagues in other subjects have not even realised that it ought to be an important aspect of their work! This has been a short-sighted attitude, which is unlikely to draw the best out of those pupils who are excellent readers *of certain sorts of texts*, but who need further insights to support their understanding of unfamiliar or more difficult forms of reading. All readers, whatever their abilities, do not naturally begin to make meaning on first contact with all sorts of texts. Even adults, who might think themselves sophisticated, experienced readers, occasionally encounter texts in unfamiliar situations which present difficulties and yield little meaning on first association. How many people on courses of further study open their recommended textbooks, read the first two paragraphs and then look back at the beginning of the page with horror and despair as they realise that they have hardly understood a word they have read!

All pupils, of whatever ability, also require ways in which they can study the texts they have read in a systematic manner, to allow them to reconstruct through writing similar texts for their own purposes. With this better understanding they should then be in a position to access a far wider range of forms and use writing more securely to aid their own learning. They will also be able to engage in writing activities to show their clearer knowledge of different ways in which texts change according to the context of their subject matter. Pupils who can construct science texts in accordance with the accepted rules of that form are likely to be thinking in a scientific way, displaying a greater all-round scientific ability, and their learning in that subject will be enhanced.

Pupils articulating their own language learning

All pupils need to be supplied with a developing *metalangue* of language use, to apply to their meaning-making activities relating to texts, and to help them take greater control of the construction of texts in those many different contexts in which they will be asked to write, both in and out of school. A *metalangue* is the linguistic knowledge a child possesses of the ways the different forms of language it employs are actually put to use. At one level it might be the recognition that sentences are denoted by capital letters at the beginning and full stops as a mark of conclusion: at the other extreme it could be the recognition of the sorts of connectives used in opinion and argument texts. More able language users take greater detailed interest in language usage, and enjoy articulating their insights and the patterns, rhythms and delights they discover at much earlier ages than their mainstream classmates. They should be supported in their efforts of learning to focus on style and syntax from the time they enter school, to take fullest advantage of their textual events.

Indeed, continuing evidence from educational research on the topic of school improvement stresses that the benefits for increasing learning, motivation and success are more apparent when pupils are actively encouraged to take a greater control of their own learning, assume more responsibility for its outcomes and improvement, and confidently comment on its content and forms. The work of Watkins, Carnell, Lodge and Whalley in 'Effective Learning' (1995) is just one recent example of a project which has identified these features as components of educational improvement. Margaret Maden, editing a set of case studies about successful educational practice, following the study undertaken by Sir Claus Moser's Commission, discovered that one of the three vital qualities which led to learning improvement was pupils' knowledge of the extent and range of their own progress, and the school being able to articulate that progress to the parents.

By being given greater knowledge of the contents of their curriculum, and the part they are expected to play in their learning, it is then reasonable to expect that pupils will be enabled to reflect more clearly on their strengths and weaknesses. This process of reflection should allow pupils to draw an accurate description of their own progress and set appropriate expectations for themselves. They should, as a consequence, then be capable of choosing targets for their projected growth. Reflection, however, will be stunted and unhelpful if it is not informed by the kind of self knowledge outlined above. To teach pupils to reflect effectively on their learning it is necessary for them to be quite secure about the contents of their programmes. 'Sharing the contents' of their learning curriculum has not been a tactic regularly employed by many teachers of English and language, with the result that, too often, pupils do not know how to improve.

One final warning I would like to mention at this point, in a period immediately before the government publishes details of the national literacy initiative, based on the model of the National Literacy Project, is of the dangers that such a departure might perpetuate. The likely rigidity of the structure for teaching literacy, through such organisational devices as the 'literacy hour', means that teachers have to be careful about the level at which pupils are placed on the programme. Because a child is chronologically expected to be in Year 3, it should not automatically follow that the able language user follows the designated Year 3 literacy programme.

Schools and their teaching staff will have to be very sensitive in ensuring that pupils do not have to mark time on work which is already known to them, and fails to extend their literacy prowess.

Chapter 2

Identifying More Able Language Users

'They too were on bloody Ginn!' (Frustrated mother of able boy, attempting to move him from a school where the staff insisted that he pass through a reading scheme, only to discover the next school she chose would treat him in the same way.)

The Reception and infant years

It is essential for everybody involved – the child, the parents and the teachers – to ensure that able language users are identified from their earliest days in school.

> It is vitally important that state schools identify their most able pupils.The idea that able pupils will always do well and do not need particular attention is discredited. Lack of effective, planned provision leads to disenchantment and under-achievement. It leads to an education system in which pupils will only succeed if they have not only the ability but also the desire to conform and do well, since they will gain little support and encouragement from teachers. (Eyre, 1997)

For schools with the youngest pupils this process has always been difficult and complicated. The assessment of language ability is a problematic undertaking at any stage of a child's education, and can never be seen as an exact science; when children have only limited ways in which to show their talents it becomes considerably harder to conduct. The requirements soon to be introduced nationally for **baseline assessment**, making early assessment judgments on Reception year children shortly after their arrival in school for comparative purposes at later stages, should give a clearer focus to the ways teachers look carefully at the linguistic potential of their new pupils.

In some circumstances the assessment will be made far easier. A few children, for instance, will already be reading when they arrive at school. This situation causes fewer problems than it once did, but it is still possible to hear horror stories about schools which demand that these pupils pass through all stages of a published reading scheme!

In the 1960s and 1970s it was common practice for children to be shepherded through the entire grading scheme (or schemes) to the very end, before becoming designated 'free readers', allowed to make personal choices from the classroom library. Some children, 'free readers' at the age of seven, were returned to the treadmill of the graded scheme on their entry to the junior school. In many schools today children still only read novels, short stories and, if they are lucky, poetry as additions to the reading scheme books. Small wonder many children fail to become readers for life. (Styles and Drummond, 1993)

Parents are usually much quicker to inform the school about their child's reading attainment these days, no longer fearing the wrath of headteachers who once claimed it was the 'job of the school' to teach initial reading. The majority of schools are now much readier to practise the essential maxim of 'beginning the child's education from the position it has already reached', not from some notional generically applied mid-point of the average ability of the intake group. My reasons for not endorsing the practice of expecting those pupils who should already be classified as 'readers' having to endure life on a commercial reading scheme are explained more fully in the chapter on Able Readers.

Those who wish to see able readers make the best progress possible also share a concern about the widespread lack of comprehensive assessment details of the actual reading ability a child might show. In huge numbers of primary schools it is not uncommon to discover that their reading records actually do little more than record the titles of texts encountered. Some really poor systems of assessment only expect teachers to colour in the appropriate level on a reading scheme pro-forma. In such circumstances there is neither reliable qualitative information to articulate how the child has developed over time, nor recommendations of what the next targets to aim for might be. This utter paucity of information about the reading achievement of the child is quite unacceptable and benefits nobody.

When schools have gone through the procedures of identifying the more able child, it then becomes necessary to put in place an effective support structure for that child's proper educational growth. As Deborah Eyre points out: 'The identification of able pupils is not an end in itself. There is only value in identifying ability if it leads to better provision ... and a better match of work to individuals.' (Eyre, 1997).

Quite a large group of children at this stage will be close to reading break-through, recognising that print carries meaning and displaying clear signs of 'readerly' behaviour. Examples of this attitude can be seen in the way they work through books in a systematic way, simulating reading or taking time to explain what is happening on separate pages; they could be looking carefully for details in illustrations and even indicating familiarity with particular letters or simple words. They usually already value books, enjoying and remembering the stories they have had read to them. All that most of these children need is a little more focused attention and help to overcome the first decoding hurdles. Their progress from that point could be rapid, given the correct support.

There will also be children who bring simple writing skills into school; they are likely to include a high proportion of the group already showing reading skills. They too will have realised that print carries meaning, and that the meaning can be sustained through the child's own text making. A very few will be capable already of composing a short paragraph of narrative or reporting text, but many more will know how to write their own names independently, and will wish to attach their own captions or labels to pictures. The problem in these circumstances is that a child might be able to write a few things in some sort of parrot fashion, but not be capable of moving on easily from that position. This child might not, in time, be thought of as more able, but the teacher should veer on the safe side and give the benefit of the doubt in the first few weeks. Who knows, the child might actually thrive by being regarded in that light!

More able young language users usually show an interest in language through their speaking and listening activities. They have a tendency to listen more carefully, possibly asking what the adult speaker means by less familiar references, and they occasionally experiment with words, or take risks with vocabulary which other mainstream children would not attempt. They display these well-developed listening skills through paying avid attention to stories. Rhona Stainthorp and Diana Hughes in research on 'young early readers' at the University of Reading suggest that powers of 'superior auditory discrimination' favour these children and contribute to beneficial employment of phonological strategies in the learning of reading (Stainthorp and Hughes, 1995). A few will have begun to speculate and think aloud, using the medium of speech to rehearse and test their ideas. Some talk through a great many of their experiences, chatting to themselves quite unselfconsciously. It is not unusual to hear them replaying encounters with teachers or other adults, which are horribly accurate in detail!

These simple criteria are straightforward enough for the majority of pupils covered by the scope of this book. They mostly reflect a high level of parental support and preparation for the demands of school. The children who display these talents are likely to have been given a clear sense of the way schools work and the expectations they have of their pupils. Their head-start will be evidenced in more significant ways than just their well-developed linguistic capacities, but it is as well to be aware that reading, writing and apparently significantly notable speaking skills are not, of themselves, reliable indicators of greater ability. Deborah Eyre warns:

> A child who has a wide vocabulary and speaks confidently may come from a home where talk is highly valued and where opportunities for discussion are numerous. She or he could appear to be very able in the early years but as schooling progresses other children may catch up. Equally a child who writes and reads early may or may not go on to be an able reader or writer. (Eyre, 1997)

With this lack of certainty in the initial judgment, teachers are likely to want to make regular checks against criteria established by the school, or have in place monitoring procedures which are sensitive to outcomes veering from the expected levels of performance. To ensure that the best coverage and identification of more able children takes place, the school cannot do better than maintain its policy of expecting the highest standards from all its pupils.

There will, however, be able children for whom the categories already described do not readily apply. A child who has shown advanced skills before arrival at school might be intimidated by the change of routine and larger groupings of new people, and fail to show the extent of the talents of which he or she is truly capable. Children can become shy or reticent in the presence of others, or unknown adults. On the other hand, there will always be a handful of pupils who have not fully enjoyed some of the preparatory experiences of their peers. The school environment might be one in which they find the necessary stimulation to excite their dormant potential. The exposure to texts and the more systematic language-based routine of the school could trigger interests the child has never before encountered. This is certainly not a time when any child should be written off, but it could be the point at which a few children will display new enthusiasms requiring careful nurturing.

Parental nomination

The belief that a few parents have in their children's abilities can often be unrealistically inflated; sometimes they are the butt of staff room jokes, or become an area of irritation. Yet they and their claims about the child just entering school have to be taken seriously. The child's preschool linguistic experiences should be of great interest to the school, and the parents will be in the best position to furnish the details of that necessary background. If the school discovers, subsequently, that the child is not performing as well as the parents have described, it will be important to discuss the different perceptions anyway. If the child's skills are all as claimed, then a partnership will have to be established to ensure that progress is maintained at the correct rate. A greater importance recently given to the notion of 'family literacy' or 'parents as co-educators' should be changing the ways schools regard their parents, and how they urge them to assist schools in their work.

The junior years

Children who have been in school for up to three years should be well known to their teachers; assessments will have been made of them in a number of ways. There might still, however, be a few children who have not, by this stage, shown their abilities to the full. So many different features trigger responses of a higher order in some youngsters: increasing maturity; growing confidence; a change to a more sympathetic teacher; participating in a project that captures the imagination;

the discovery of a book which stimulates ideas as no other has done, are some examples.

I would like to suggest that the tests which children encounter, either statutory or because the school deems them necessary, are not in themselves a reliable guide to greater ability. Reading tests, particularly, are very limited in what they uncover about the child undertaking them, beyond confirming the teacher's own judgment. The reading ability of any child should be described over a far larger range of features than any test ever embraced. They are not, on the whole, designed to identify more able readers! Later in this book I shall make a case for claiming that only in schools where there are clearly formulated and shared policies about reading and writing, and broadly based assessment practices, will genuine support for able language users be properly available. The same criteria also need to exist to identify these pupils in the first place. 'Schools become more effective in identifying able children as they get better at providing for them.' (Eyre, 1997)

There have also been plenty of instances where children have been considered able yet, surprisingly, have failed to score significantly well on apparently standardised tests. There are a number of reasons why children might not live up to the expectations adults might have of them in these circumstances. Ralph Tabberer, a former Deputy Director at the NFER, has told the story of the pilot testing exercise, using a flag shape outline to explore some conceptual knowledge. Children were invited to add 'two lines of symmetry' within this outline. One pupil responded with:

| symmetry | symmetry | symmetry | symmetry |
| symmetry | symmetry | symmetry | symmetry |

Some pupils, interested in the possibilities of language, do not hesitate in interpreting all instructions literally; well beyond the scope of the test deviser's intentions.

Pupils will be in a better position to offer more evidence of their linguistic skills by the time they reach primary school. They will have had opportunities for reading a wider range of texts; they will have been given chances to write in a broader selection of text types; and they will have attempted composition in different styles and given notice of the accuracy of their written efforts. I mention all of these areas because 'more able' in respect of language talent can be applied to many aspects of a child's work.

A pupil might be thought of as a 'good reader', but this classification is simply unhelpful unless the notion of 'good' applied to reading has been broken down into clearer elements. Is the reader a voracious one, ready to tackle anything available? Is the reader a keen one, settling down to read, without any urging, whatever the material? Is the reader one who enjoys the challenge of difficult texts? Who draws on an excellent repertoire for comparative purposes? Able to interpret the text at many levels? Capable of reading between the lines? These sorts of consideration should be the starting point of setting up criteria for making assessments of reading competence.

A comparable set of questions can be applied to the 'good writer'. Does the child who picks up a pen readily, and gets on with his work, qualify as 'good'? Does the child who spells accurately and writes neatly qualify as 'good'? Does 'good' mean the child who attempts new structural devices, but does not always present writing neatly and carefully? Might 'good' really only apply to a writer who is wholly in control of the forms being used?

One of the most difficult problems to resolve in respect of identifying 'good' writers is to do with the scope of the opportunities writers are actually given to show their prowess. If the tasks they are given are not challenging or able to provide a sufficiently secure platform on which a potentially good writer can perform, then the work is more likely to be moribund or commonplace. Many writers do not have worthwhile horizons opened to them because their teachers are unaware of what, given the right support and motivation, they might be capable of achieving. Only where teachers are preparing for possible writing outcomes of real quality can writers fully indicate their true skills. Robert Protherough reminds us of the very real problems of identifying more able writers:

> Writing is heavily, indeed dominantly, influenced by the situation in which it is carried out, the purpose for which it is written and the topic. The first version of the national curriculum for English summed this up in the words 'language competence is dependent on the task: children will show different ability on tasks of different kinds.' (Protherough in (ed.) Goodwyn, 1995)

The secondary school

There are some pupils who pass through the primary school system without their linguistic potential being fully appreciated and exploited. These pupils could have been quiet and undemonstrative, only making apparent to their teachers the texts read in the classroom and writing accurate but undistinguished pieces in the sort of setting described in the previous section. Because English is a specialist subject in the secondary school they enjoy different opportunities to show their talents to teachers who are usually able to support and challenge them, in learning contexts which allow them to grow. But the act of transfer to secondary school is not in itself a guarantee that they will, even then, be properly identified. The department has to have in place an assessment system able to distinguish the fullest range of qualities displayed by its incoming pupils. More importantly, the department has to be prepared to recognise what its incoming pupils might be capable of achieving, based on their previous experiences.

I have heard heads of secondary English departments deny that the pupils in their incoming cohort are able to achieve Level 5 or even Level 6 at the end of Key Stage 2! Such views represent a tiny minority of teachers, but that they have been expressed is alarming. They point to a poor relationship between the local primary schools and the accepting secondary department. They also perpetuate the argument that can still be heard in a few isolated quarters, that the child's English/ language education does not properly begin until the start of secondary schooling. I once inserted the allegorical story (in Figure 6.11, p.97), written by a Year 5 pupil into a batch of Year 9 scripts being considered for moderation purposes by a group of secondary heads of English. One colleague refused to believe, at the end of the exercise – during which the piece had been favourably regarded – that it could have been written by a pupil still in the primary school!

Many English departments have excellent relationships with their feeder schools, having made worthwhile transfer arrangements which allow pupils' most favourable linguistic achievements to be recognised. Written examples of different text types, reviews of recently read books, and notes referring to pupils' speaking attainment, can be enormously helpful for the receiving department if they are structured to yield real information and are taken seriously. Such relationships will depend on mutual trust and confidence; when both sorts of school know important details about the work, approaches and attitudes of the other. One feature of transfer which I have regularly been depressed about in recent years has been to do with the reading programmes of secondary English departments. Too often they have assigned pupils a common reading curriculum in Year 7, depending more on the available texts than the actual needs or attainment of the pupils concerned. Better developed liaison activity with a focus on reading would have prevented this situation and allowed the English teachers to match resources and challenge more appropriately.

Chapter 3

What the School Can Do:
Preparation, Policy and Parents

Infant schools

If schools are intending to make a difference to the progress and growth of the more able language users, they have to be properly prepared to receive them. All schools should expect that there will be at least one more able child in every intake, but it would be preferable to be ready for far more. In some areas of the country, where children are brought up in relative comfort, where planned and frequent domestic and social language experiences have been commonplace, there is likely to be high proportion of able pupils in each school intake, displaying early reading, writing or speaking talents. The greater the number of such pupils there are in a single school, the easier it should be to care for them appropriately. A large group should remind the staff of its presence more obviously, and the group itself is able to be used as a resource to support all its members. Unfortunately, this situation does not always prevail.

Even in those catchment areas where indicators, such as free school meals, suggest that fewer children enjoy early encounters with books, stories or the ways of language which advantage learning, there will be pupils who, for reasons impossible to explain, discover and explore a fascination with texts beyond the ordinary. (English literature and autobiographical works are full of instances of children from socially disadvantaged backgrounds who discovered an early love of words, and made considerable strides because of that asset.) If the school believes there is a strong likelihood that some children on the roll have wide-ranging, genuine linguistic potential, then it will actually make real efforts to look out for them. It is not necessary that these children will also have shown outstanding mathematical or technological potential: the signs of more able linguistic abilities are themselves quite enough to demand a particular sort of attention, and to set into motion a support programme. Just as the school should be taking its responsibilities seriously for those who will require special support to enable fuller access to the whole curriculum, so it should be anticipating the needs of this other group, who require more than the average provision of any well-planned learning course.

As it happens, those children who possess more advanced linguistic skills are likely to be making significantly better progress in other subjects of the curriculum anyway, especially in those subjects with a heavy writing and reading content.

Junior and secondary schools

Junior and secondary schools should also be seeking the evidence of those more able pupils arriving from their feeder schools. What is certain, especially at the stressful time of school transfer, is that pupils will not step forward and demand attention of their own volition, although sometimes their parents might make a case on the child's behalf! Yet it is vital that children who have been reading books at a particular level, or across a broad range, or who have shown a capability in certain types of writing, should be allowed to continue to make progress from the stage they have already reached.

Many secondary school English departments make little special provision for individual talent at the beginning of Key Stage 3, setting whole-class tasks without much opportunity for 'extension' reading activities. A few departments expect all the pupils to engage with reading texts which are too undemanding for the majority, in the mistaken belief that as many appear not to be confident readers they will be able to cope with a relatively simple book. Imagine the frustration of those readers who are capable of tackling more complex books than most of their classmates in this situation! I have met many pupils in classrooms who complain strongly about the simple reading they have to endure in lessons, conducted at a pace which is numbing.

There are few excuses for able pupils to transfer to secondary school without having already been identified as possessing certain skills in advance of their classmates. Only if a child has been a genuinely late developer, or displays previously unseen talents in his (or her) new surroundings, would there be good reasons for not passing on information about his recognised abilities. Yet each school year, enormous numbers of more able language users pass from primary to secondary schools without triggering a properly designed set of support and challenge activities. Only where the dispatching and receiving schools have actually focused upon this issue as being worthy of real attention will an effective case be made for transfer information to include clear evidence of the child's special accomplishments. Only where two schools have shared a notion of what 'more able' might mean in relation to their usual language expectations will real identification be taking place. Only where a school has mature policy in position will it have the necessary prompts to act on that information and integrate the pupil at the level commensurate with his talents.

Policy for the more able language user

If the school is looking out for more able language users then it makes sense to draw up a policy to outline a consistent approach to be followed by all staff.

Teachers often groan at the thought of yet more policy documentation to devise and take notice of, but if a problem has been specified then it must be addressed in formal terms to allow all participants to articulate the same aims. To support these identified pupils aged 5 to 11 most effectively, a primary school should write a whole-school policy which helps identify those who are being selected for special support, and sets out ways in which their progress can be satisfactorily monitored and sustained. In a secondary school the separate departments should adopt their own approaches to policy-making, but these take on greater significance and power if they relate to a whole-school overview. Whatever the school context, the English department should have its own strategies, outlining broad-ranging criteria for identification and challenge, already prepared for their more able incoming pupils.

It is important that policies make allowances for those pupils who, at different stages in their school lives, could well show unexpected insights and capabilities at any time, as they come across new materials or texts which stimulate them in ways leading to new understanding and attainment. The most important reason for having policy guidelines already in place is to bring about a school or departmental ethos where pupils are expected to fulfil their potential, whatever their abilities. A further benefit will become apparent for schools or departments who have demanding expectations of certain pupils through such policy guidance; other pupils will want to join in the facilities being offered, or enjoy similar challenge, and the likelihood is that the attainment of a wider group will be enhanced as a result of this extended interest.

The policy making does not have to be lengthy or complicated. The policy document itself can be brief. Deborah Eyre offers an outline pro forma in the appendix of her book *Able Children in Ordinary Schools* (Eyre, 1997), which has twelve simple sections. More effective than any elaborate policy is the genuinely shared implementation of a way of working, bringing about collaborative practice by the team of teachers. It would be preferable if one of the staff is designated the task of monitoring the policy; not in itself an onerous task, but one which could lead to regular reminders about consistent provision. That person might also be the first point of contact for identified pupils, offering a mentoring role.

Any policy addressing the more able should contain a section pointing to the extra provision those pupils ought to be receiving through their studies or beyond the formal classroom. Particular examples will be explored in greater detail in the sections on more able readers and writers later in the book, but I would like to mention some general points relating to 'differentiation'.

Differentiation

'Differentiation' is a term often heard in education, one which appears regularly in planning documentation, but is an elusive phenomenon, difficult to find in practice. It is even more difficult to trace in English. One of the problems about differentiation is that it seems to be interpreted **in different ways in difficult** situations: setting pupils by ability, for instance, could be seen as one form of differentiation; fast-tracking pupils, allowing talented younger pupils to work with those in the school who are older, is another. Most teachers employ some forms of differentiation at different times, often in the way they frame questions in the classroom, and in the way they select those pupils who answer them. The marking process is another obvious example of differentiation; teachers select the most appropriate feedback to their pupils, based on what they know of each learner's capacity to benefit from it. As teachers talk to their pupils, they are dealing with each individual in a unique way, cajoling or encouraging, depending on the teacher's knowledge of the pupil.

The definition proposed in this book, which lends itself readily to integration in policy documentation is:

- Differentiation is recognising individual differences and trying to find institutional strategies to take account of them.

This understanding of the word should help to eliminate the rather fruitless discussion which regularly arises when differentiation is considered, about whether it involves 'differentiation by outcome', or 'differentiation by task', or 'differentiation by resource'. Outcomes need to be planned for, the range of possible tasks explored and the appropriate resources provided for all learners, whatever their ability. Of course, there will regularly be occasions when opportunities which have not been scrupulously planned arise in lessons, and teachers may often be thrilled with the quality of unexpected outcomes which are the results. Yet these exceptional moments, themselves requiring great skill to maximise, do not diminish the need for careful planning still essential to bring together those factors which are necessary to ensure the best possible outcomes of the learning encounter.

Perhaps a less fussy way of thinking about differentiation is by expecting teachers always to include the notion of possible extension in any planning they set up for their groups. Tasks are approached from the premise that:

- 'everybody can' achieve a defined base-line outcome;
- 'some pupils should' be able to attain at a rather higher level;
- 'a few pupils might' achieve the most notable results.

It is not necessary to know who will eventually be assigned to each of these groups at the outset.

There will be occasions when pupils surprise their teachers. What is important in this arrangement is that pupils who have reached the base-line have another layer of challenge to explore. There are always further tasks – 'another chapter to read', 'an extra comparison to make', 'a closer look at', 'considering the text represented in another medium', 'a more explicit explanation to be given' – to probe in English and language studies. Too often exercises and assignments are set in classrooms which some pupils have already understood and mastered. The most valuable extension challenge the teacher can provide in those circumstances is to move the learner into a 'what next?' way of thinking.

Parents

Most parents will be delighted to know their child has been identified as one of the more able language users by their school. They will be even more impressed to see a programme already in place, which it is likely they will want to support, and in which, the chances are, they will want to participate. The sort of ability being described in this book is one which children can 'take home'! It does not depend on specialised teaching at all times or mean that difficult resources have to be provided, and willing parents can be easily accommodated into playing a supportive part in its development.

Nearly every adult is in a position at least to ask questions about a text being read, even if they do not know its contents. Indeed, establishing what is taking place and how well that is being understood is a most suitable starting point for conversation. If adults can be shown how to extend their child's understanding of the text which is being read, or offer encouragement or prompts in a variety of ways to a text being written, or spend a short time discussing a topic being explored, then the parents can become genuine partners. Book lists can help parents choose texts, either from the library or to purchase. Short booklets containing suggestions to assist parents in playing a fuller supportive part should be the very least result of policy making.

These same resources are just as important for parents with children in the secondary school as they are for parents with infant children. Ironically, it is often with the older children that parents have the more difficult task; older children can be harder to make contact with and parents are usually less sure about the projects or tasks in which their children are involved. If their children are not always prepared to show their full talents in the school setting, because of the pressure they might be feeling from their peers, it is essential that they share their ideas, insights and critical skills with people in a home setting, where they might feel more comfortable.

Extra-curricular provision

If a school or a department has gone to the trouble of writing a policy to deal with more able language users, it is likely that the staff involved will be more prepared to consider the different ways in which the pupils they identify can benefit from the extension activities that will result, both in and out of lessons. A few schools I have known have made extra provision for individual pupils, sometimes linking them with others in different classes or those in different years. Other schools have made special arrangements for a broader group of pupils, including their most able, but not exclusively designed for them.

Those pupils supported individually are often given resources such as booklists, or allowed extra time, during school breaks or at the end of the day, for further conversations. Sometimes they are invited to join groups of older pupils for particular lessons, or activities such as theatre visits or reading/writing workshops.

The able pupils who are supported in a broader framework often benefit from special 'theme days' which are organised for a larger group. One school I know regularly organises a 'Shakespeare Day' for Year 8 pupils who show linguistic aptitude, to study a chosen text in a number of contexts. Of course, a few schools assign their able pupils to ability sets from time of entry (which does not, of itself solve the problems of properly supporting the more able language users), or during subsequent years, but some schools draw their able pupils together during the school year for particular events. Visiting authors, poets and drama groups are often used for these purposes.

In Oxfordshire, during the days when it was possible to arrange centrally based events, Peter Thomas, then Head of English at Wheatley Park School, and David Draper, Head of English at St Birinus School, Didcot, used to organise annual Talented Young Writers in Oxfordshire Schools workshop weekends. Schools were invited to nominate participants, who worked alongside a group of teachers, including practising authors, at a residential centre. Their published results were genuinely impressive collections of writing. Recently, the English departments of schools in the West network of the county have invited David Draper to lead a day's course for more able language users. He has given them tasks such as the beginning of a story to complete and collaborative drama direction, through which to explore and develop their abilities. Other local education authorities have offered similar activities during school holidays, recognising that able language users need to have opportunities to see others at work, and the chance to learn from them.

Chapter 4

What the School Can Do:
A View of Language Learning

For a primary school or an English department to make a real difference to the achievement of more able users of language, the staff involved must have a shared approach to learning in the subject from a position which has been articulated and understood by the whole team. Teachers must be confident that they have a clear sense of how it is possible for pupils to improve before they can plan for that eventuality. During the past few years schools have been challenged to engage in explaining this process more fully and naturally, to satisfy the demands of senior management, OFSTED and Local Education Authority advisers and inspectors, amongst others. Many groups of teachers have also felt it necessary to discuss these issues and publish their interpretation of them because they actually believe this collaborative understanding leads to more effective teaching and learning organisations.

Background

The nature and content of the subject called 'English' has changed a good deal during the last few years, and that change shows no sign of slowing down. The relationship of the subject with different notions of literacy, for instance, the stuff of current debate and national policy-making, make it even more necessary for primary teachers and teachers of English in secondary schools to explore carefully what they think they are teaching and attempting to achieve in their classrooms. As I write, proposals for a national literacy strategy are being prepared, which will mean primary schools having to reconsider – yet again – how they will plan, teach and assess curriculum programmes in language, literacy and English. Virtually all schools will have to emphasise the importance of literacy through the imposition of a 'literacy hour', yet this extra attention to one aspect of the subject will still not in itself provide a full 'English' curriculum. Schools will still have to make further provision for areas of literary study not covered in the national literacy scheme.

When I was head of an English department in the second half of the 1970s, it was possible for my staff and myself to select favourite or familiar texts from the shelves in the English stockroom almost at random, and deal with them in any manner we wished, as long as they were felt to be suitable in terms of challenge and interest for the pupils concerned. An acceptable programme for our younger pupils, not at that stage on examination courses, was one which covered a proper proportion of narrative reading and writing, a few poems and the occasional play, with perhaps a little non-fiction study and some opportunity for speaking. What I did in my classroom was not systematically complemented elsewhere in the department, although we regularly 'borrowed' good ideas. The sort of English programme encountered by the pupils was entirely dependent on the whims and interests of individual teachers. We read books with our pupils, and engaged in some study to bring about better 'comprehension', but we had little notion of how to make them better readers or writers. Progression was not planned and any sense of 'entitlement' was not part of our collaborative thinking, although during my time in the post the department was increasingly urged to look more closely at its aims and objectives. We might not have been in the vanguard of English thinking, but we were regarded as a successful department and typical of many at that time.

I wish that I had been asked the sorts of questions about the nature and *purpose* of our work that are now taken for granted in all schools. I know that the quality, intent and growth of what we planned for our pupils would have been more carefully focused and worthwhile. I would also hope that we could have then, together, constructed a curriculum which spanned all five years of the secondary stage, recognising ways that pupils grew intellectually and linguistically, and thus have accommodated all their needs more successfully.

In 1970, when I began teaching, virtually all secondary English teachers were proud to inform those who asked them about the nature and content of their work that 'literature' was at the centre of all they undertook. They read selected shared texts with their pupils in their classrooms, set a considerable number of comprehension exercises based on countless extracts taken from familiar works, and made up essay titles – often unrelated to any other work taking place, and certainly not intended to explore particular text-types – for their pupils to write either in the class or at home. Teachers then marked the essays relentlessly, too regularly covering pages of writing with red annotations and corrections, taking full control of the assessment procedure. An alarming number of teachers also expected their pupils to wade through endless grammar exercises published in books that assured teacher and student that, by studying the separate components of language in isolation, the students would become better, more fluent and accurate writers. On the whole, they did not.

The picture in primary schools was no more enlightened. Thousands of classes of children endured exercises of English 'drill'; filling in gaps of missing words, underlining 'parts of speech' and writing compositions on 'improving topics' in an exercise still often referred to as 'creative writing' (a term used, I believe to differentiate this particular form – perhaps a fictional story or a description – from 'practical' or 'transactional' writing, which was used to report on real events). In case readers are inclined to accuse me of exaggeration, I offer one illustration from a book (R. F. Eagle, *Stride Ahead in English 2*, Wheaton, 1964) I found being used in a classroom in 1996:

BE TIDY IN YOUR APPEARANCE!
Here are fifteen sentences. Ten are sensible. Five are silly. Write out only those sentences which are sensible.

Comb your hair, when necessary, during the day.
Keep your nails trimmed and clean.
Keep your teeth in good condition, by cleaning them frequently.
If you look in the mirror, and see that your face is dirty, wash the mirror.
Wash your hands and face as often as may be necessary.
If you take your coat off, drop it on the floor where people can use it for a door-mat
[... and so on!]

Few teachers could have described how real learning was taking place through this sort of work, and 'getting better' usually meant dealing more fluently with harder exercises of the same order. My wife has an exercise book from her primary school in 1965 which contains work and exercises remarkably similar to my son's experiences in 1995!

Towards the end of the 1970s and into the 1980s, secondary teachers gradually discarded the books of extracts with their companion comprehension exercises, rejecting the grammar drills at the same time, as they moved towards a more 'empathetic' study of literature. They also wanted to make their study of texts increasingly relevant for a broader group of pupils.

Most of us have encountered the conventional 'Law Court' approach to literature which expects the reader to argue a case with high skill in a detached way, making constant reference to evidence and comment. 'Macbeth is not entirely evil. Discuss' invites detailed argument backed by reference and quotation to support one's point of view, all conducted in a scholarly style and essay format. Such an approach can be deeply rewarding and engrossing, and can lead to further insights into the text and into the reader, but our conversations with teachers suggest that this approach is 'at its best' for the mature and able. (Hayhoe and Parker, 1984)

This new approach gave greater emphasis to an understanding of what it might 'feel like' to be a character in a book, or to exploring how the reader might react if caught up in a similar situation. Diaries, letters and contemporary newspaper reports capturing the details of the events in the narrative were more regularly set as writing tasks, in more realistic contexts, for pupils. They allowed the pupil readers to show their understanding of the narrative texts in a more engaging manner than the formerly popular style of detached explanatory essay – far more suited to capable writers. This way of working in English classrooms accorded closely with the 'personal growth' view of the subject, which a majority of secondary English teachers claimed to be their most favoured model of teaching in a small-scale study (Goodwyn, 1992).

From the 1980s into the 1990s there has been further discernible change in the way that the majority of English teachers approach the subject. Even with the better focus provided by the National Curriculum orders, most teachers have become far less sure about how they describe the nature of their work and the relationship of the different parts of their subject. Some of this uncertainty has arisen because of considerable political interference, leading to large changes in the content of the English curriculum over a very short period of time. An evolving academic background, owing much to the work of Halliday, exploring how pupils learn in socio-linguistic contexts, has supplied new dimensions of framing the subject which teachers of English have continued to incorporate into their work. Critical theories about the reading process, such as 'reader-response', 'deconstruction', 'structuralism' and 'post-structuralism' have also had impact on the ways texts are studied. An approach approximating to the 'personal growth' model is still important to many, and the close, often trusting relationship that children have with their English teachers bears witness to this continued rapport. At the same time a growing awareness of how communication technologies and culture, as represented in increasingly powerful media forms, were having enormous effect on the ways young people make sense of their world meant that the 'cultural analysis' stance was also gaining ground. Simultaneously, a very recent political focus on 'literacy' has begun to shift the 'English' landscape yet again, and during the next few years a stronger emphasis on the study of language as the building material of texts will move to centre stage of the subject. English teachers are still, rightly, concerned with the teaching and promotion of literature. Statutorily, they are obliged to give this aspect of the subject enormous attention with a very demanding programme of reading to satisfy. Most, however, now recognise that the primacy they would once have claimed for literary study has diminished.

Literature texts comprise only a portion of the sorts of reading and writing matter that teachers of English in secondary schools feel they ought to be studying and opening up for their pupils. Even the term 'literature' is far more difficult to pin down than it was, especially through the way it is interpreted in schools.

> The uncertain status and being of the literary text – a primary object of English – raises in turn the problem of the identity of the subject. The identity of English has been to a significant extent founded on the idea of the literary text, and on the related idea of the value of a literary education. One interestingly provocative thing about this, though, is that the literary text has changed its identity through the years. In effect, it is notoriously impossible to define what literature is – or what the limits of literature might be. (Peim, 1995)

The frequency of the word 'text' in a book such as this points to a changing awareness of what teachers of language and literacy, in primary and secondary education, now feel they need to address to prepare their pupils more completely for their lives in and beyond school. No longer is their concern solely for 'the book' – of a particular sort – but with all published materials, including magazines, newspapers, video texts, CDs, logos and computer games with which their pupils are increasingly familiar (usually more familiar than their teachers!). They must, of course, give primary stress to the process of reading the written word for meaning, but we have come to understand that the ways 'writing' can be read is dependent on the context in which it appears, the original purpose of the writing, and the realisation that it might not mean the same things to different audiences reading it in different ways. One single, teacher-mediated reading of a text is now rarely promoted.

English teachers in secondary schools have also become more aware that their pupils need to be able to read in a variety of ways to be properly equipped to deal with the full extent of a diverse school curriculum. Their primary counterparts, teaching a number of subjects in the same room, have long been aware of this need, but the ways of assisting children to use a variety of texts for learning at Key Stage 2 have not always been fully developed. So the breadth of reading materials now regarded as necessary content of the English programme continues to grow; partly evident in the extent of non-narrative study required in the current GCSE syllabuses.

Change in the English curriculum can be seen too in the ways teachers are gradually beginning to approach the teaching of writing. Twenty years ago, the writing expected in secondary schools was extremely limited in range and was of a sort not usually continued by pupils after they had finished full-time study. In primary schools HMI noted:

> In the course of their day to day work children devoted much time to writing ... Narrative and descriptive writing in prose were almost universal, writing associated with topic work often entailed excessive copying from reference books, the incidence being highest with 11 year old children. Although the older, abler children were capable of using writing to argue a case, to express opinions, or to draw conclusions most of them had little experience of those kinds of writing. (DES, 1990)

Increasingly during the last few years, and certainly since the introduction of the National Curriculum (which has itself absorbed some of the better findings of such initiatives as The Writing Project), far more concern has been given to the *purposes* of writing and the *audiences*, real or imaginary, for whom that writing is intended. Put simply, there is now a recognition that there is no point in undertaking a writing exercise unless it is about something worth considering, it is designed to bring about a genuine reaction on the intended reader, and that learning of some sort – even if it is about the writing process itself – takes place as a consequence.

Schools are waking up to the fact that most of the writing they have been demanding until the present has failed to meet most of these simple objectives. The National Literacy Strategy will certainly make clear to primary schools that they must rethink entirely the scope and extent of their writing curriculum, and it can only be hoped that secondary schools will quickly emulate that lead.

It follows that if teachers recognise that writing has a *purpose*, it should be possible to discover, through careful analysis of existing pieces of writing, published or hand-written, how well the intended or suggested purposes for it have been met. 'How successful has this piece of writing been?' is the straightforward question which pupils should be assisted to ask on their own behalf. The texts deemed as successful can then serve as 'models', on which pupils can base the construction of their own texts of a similar kind. If they can then extend or improve on those forms, to show their increasing control of them, so much the better, but they have to be able to show that they can write quite clearly in that particular form in the context required in the first place.

Whilst still in the early stages of learning to write, in the Reception Year and Year 1 of infant school, young pupils should be shown what to construct, based on simple examples, to familiarise them with the available writing repertoire. There is not a hierarchical structure of writing, beginning, for instance, with simple narrative in the early years and ending with argument/opinion discourse in Key Stage 4. All pupils should be given opportunities to learn about the full range of text types, at appropriate levels, from the start.

> We would argue that children should be introduced to non-fiction texts and how to learn from them from their earliest days in school. Indeed, the new curriculum orders for English (DfE, 1995) are quite explicit in their requirements for teachers to provide children with learning experiences, both in reading and writing, that are based on non-fiction material. (Wray and Lewis, 1997)

The ultimate goal of this work should be to empower all pupils to make their own choices of text, dependent on purpose, audience and context, in all the writing tasks they tackle. If pupils are able to articulate the text type they have chosen to their teachers, because it fulfils purposes they have identified, impressing upon the reader some learning that has happened, or a particular effect, then the learning of writing has been well-planned and focused. Teachers of English are beginning to understand this rationale of writing rather better than their counterparts in other subjects, who still tend to control the writing they require too closely, failing to make writing implicit in the learning of their subjects and offering a limited range of forms through which pupils can practise. In actual fact, OFSTED evidence shows that far too much copying of teacher or text book writing takes place in virtually the whole curriculum in too many classrooms. Able writers do not grow in these situations.

Language learning over the past decade has been helped by the increased emphasis on the separate components of **reading**, **writing**, **speaking** and

listening. The attention accorded to considering the essential differences in these forms of communication in National Curriculum documentation, and the requirement to assess them separately, has meant a more balanced approach to the English curriculum in all phases of schooling. Previously, the pronounced bias towards writing was evident in most schools, with speaking and listening rarely achieving proper recognition or attention. Yet whilst better balance has been achieved, the subsequent increased separateness of the forms has regularly led to inadequate or ill-informed planning based on a view of language which is not borne out in real language use. It is impossible, for example, to separate writing from reading, and quite difficult to read for understanding without at some time speaking to others about the insights being discovered, or listening to the responses of others, from which our own meanings can be made or modified. Language learning operates in social spheres, which are constantly interweaving discourses in written and spoken forms, interpreted through reading and listening.

Schools have to make the relationship between reading and writing unequivocally explicit. These language domains have to be understood as the reverse of each other (see Figure 4.1). The talk and listening which takes place as a consequence of studying texts (spoken language, of all sorts, itself being a form of text) can then be seen as a sort of binding mechanism.

Figure 4.1

A possible way of regarding language growth and development in school planning

The adoption of a more balanced English curriculum, which emphasises learning of language and literacy skills in relation to a broad range of texts, means that schools will also have to think again about what 'linguistic growth' might entail. Whilst the ability to read is still utterly vital, that skill is now seen as a more extensive need for children to **make meaning** on a much broader platform of language experiences. Being able merely to read – that is, to decode the words of a text – was never regarded as being an acceptable educational tool, and is no longer recognised as being enough to satisfy modern literacy demands, or sufficient to make real progress in the school, or any other institutional, system. Similarly, as necessary as it is for pupils to write – making marks on paper with pen or pencil, or on screen with a word processor – they need a better understanding of the processes of, and the power to bring about, the **construction of texts**, drawing on the fullest knowledge they can acquire of the way texts carry and convey meaning. Of course, to construct a real variety of texts they will have had to develop their skills in making meaning from other, already existing, texts to use as models for their own. (My 12-year-old son regularly uses a computer to do his homework. He draws information, written text and graphics, together from different sources, edits, changes layouts and prints a final copy. He is capable of printing thousands of copies of his work and could be regarded as a publisher. He is accomplished in much more than merely writing; yet in a great deal of this activity he is self-taught.)

The two elements of language construction and understanding are continually interacting. As text constructors we write or speak, to convey meaning: to deconstruct, or make meaning from the texts which have either been constructed by ourselves or others, we read or we listen. To think of pupils as **text constructors**, or **text deconstructors/text meaning makers** is to rethink, fundamentally, the processes required by language learners to make powerful and effective texts of their own, and articulate what they know about them. Able language users need to be thought of in this way, to extend their own sense of language knowledge, but so do their more average classmates.

One final component to include in this view of language learning is that of the pupil as **reflective language user**. To bring about real language learning improvement, as shown earlier in the book, pupils must be able, increasingly, to recognise the types of discourses in which they are taking part, engaging with or initiating. The more able users of language are those who can call on a fuller repertoire of language application, make progressively independent decisions about the features on which they wish to call, and realistically anticipate the sorts of reactions they are likely to bring about in others, through the style, vocabulary or voice of the texts they have constructed.

> If assessment is to be effective generally, it needs to involve and include pupils themselves, and in English, a subject that makes pre-eminent both the person and the personal, it is absolutely paramount. (Goodwyn, 1995)

To aid those who are already significantly developing their powers of language in school, at all stages, teachers have to be in a position to know how to support the next stages of development. The questions 'what next' or 'where next', already rehearsed earlier, have to be continually asked of even the work of successful text makers, or meaning makers, at whatever stage of schooling they have reached.

Teachers should be able to help their pupils call on further ways of making meaning, delving deeper into the layers of meaning a text contains ('might there be other reasons for thinking that?'), or assisting them in challenging the intentions that are guiding the manner and extent of their text construction ('why did you use that phrase in that place?'). An assessment system sensitive to the language learning needs outlined above will then alert pupils to the areas in which they have to improve.

An overview of language and literacy learning

A statement of language and literacy learning which I have been using frequently with schools as an attempt to bring coherence to this difficult area is:

> Language and literacy learning is provided for the *empowerment* of pupils, by assisting them to make meaning through the development of a range of *critical skills*, brought about as a result of increased familiarity with many different sorts of texts.
>
> This study is designed to extend pupils' confidence in and control of *a variety of linguistic domains*, such as reading, writing, speaking and listening, enabling them to be discerning about and to participate fully and appropriately in *a complete range of possible discourses*, whatever their *contexts*. It is also intended to encourage pupils' ability to reflect on the place of language in *creating the identity of individuals*, and the ways in which it is employed to explore and create *aesthetic and metaphoric ideas*.
>
> A vital part of this study is the recognition of the *relationship between language, thinking and learning* in all areas of the school curriculum and beyond.

The separate, italicised parts of this statement deserve further explanation.

Empowerment

The goal of language/literacy education is for pupils to take more and more control of their language and literacy encounters. There is a general agreement in our society that being 'literate' is a necessary ingredient of full personal empowerment, as if that *literacy* is a single state which can be bestowed on someone. In fact, there are many literacies: merely being able to read words on a page or a screen is not in itself sufficient. To be able to read and take full sense from certain sorts of fiction texts demands a set of skills which are not always helpful to pupils confronting information texts, where other skills are have to be drawn on.

> Narrative is very definitely the dominant genre both in children's reading and writing and, where efforts are made to enhance and deepen children's responses to text, these seem to be confined to experiences with narratives of one kind or another. Yet it has been quite forcibly pointed out by Martin (1989), among several others, that the bulk of adult experience with texts involves interactions with genres other than narrative. (Wray and Lewis, 1997)

There are also *media literacies* – those which allow audiences to 'read' or better understand, for instance, televisual images, film structure and framing; the actual matter of what is being 'sold' in an advertisement; the layout, contents and narrative devices of newspapers – the ways that our lives and culture are represented and reflected back to us. Children also have to learn another set of practices associated with operating and finding their way round computers and their programs, which can be as diverse in nature as are many different sorts of books. Being knowledgeable about and able to administer a degree of control over these disparate but linked literacies are skills that young people require to develop real understanding of the worlds in which they operate.

Critical skills

Pupils need to learn from school how to confront and 'interrogate' texts, whatever their nature and in whatever medium, oral or visual, they are perceived. The *Language in the National Curriculum* project, which was conducted in England from 1989 to 1993, as a result of the *Kingman Report* (DES, 1988), gave enormous attention to the ways pupils could be assisted in engaging in active analysis. The framework (Figure 4.2) is part of the project's final publication, which incorporated some of the best language training materials that were ever produced, although LINC's findings were never officially published. This framework provides an excellent starting point for discovering the central meaning of many sorts of text, printed or published in a variety of forms. Some readers might think of critical skills as those abilities which enable students to discover the layers of meaning in literary texts: the term, as used here, relates to that skill, but so much more.

A variety of linguistic domains

This grand phrase is a way of attempting to indicate that language experiences and interactions take place in a huge variety of ways, which are not simply explained in terms of just reading, writing, speaking and listening; although they are the most convenient way of separating language activities. 'Speaking', for instance, tells us little about the nuances and tonal qualities of utterances, or the body 'language' which might accompany them. 'Reading', as I have already mentioned, is becoming a term meaning much more than just decoding print on a page. Pupils constantly and effortlessly read immense numbers of symbols beyond mere letters in their daily interactions, naturally making meaning from them.

A complete range of possible discourses

This phrase is meant to include any form of language being communicated or perceived by anybody at any time: oral, aural, print-based, broadcast or electronic.

A FRAMEWORK FOR LOOKING AT TEXTS

1. WHO SPEAKS THIS TEXT?
(Is there an 'I' or a 'we' in the text? What kind of voice is this? Does the writer address me directly, or through an adopted "persona"?)

2. WHO IS BEING SPOKEN TO?
(Is there a 'you' in the text? What kind of audience is being addressed, and how can we tell? Am I prepared to include myself in this audience?)

3. WHERE DOES THIS TEXT COME FROM?
(What do we know about when, why and how it was produced? Does the text itself disclose these things? What status does it have? What values does the text assume?)

4. WHAT KIND OF TEXT IS THIS?
(What other texts does this remind me of? What form does it take? What recognisable conventions has the writer adopted?)

5. WHAT DOES THE TEXT WANT?
(What do I deduce about the writer's intentions? Are these intentions openly stated? What kind of reading does this text invite?)

6. WHAT DOES THIS TEXT MEAN TO ME?
(What are my motives as a reader of this text? How have I chosen to interpret it? Do I share its values? What thoughts has it prompted?)

You might like to ask all these questions of the page you are holding ...

The resources of written texts
In discussing these questions, it might be helpful to consider some of the detailed *rhetorical choices* which writers make:-

PRESENTATIONAL: (e.g. choices of lay-out, type-face, illustration)
ORGANISATIONAL: (e.g. choices of narrative, logical, metrical or figurative pattern)
GRAMMATICAL: (e.g. choices of tense, mode, person, syntax, punctuation)
LEXICAL: (e.g. choices of vocabulary, idiom, metaphor)

Figure 4.2

Quite simply, the intention is that no situation or encounter should ultimately be beyond the learner, who will either understand the characteristics of the circumstance, and be able to participate in like or appropriate manner, or reach for skills which lead to further engagement. Too frequently, pupils do not know how to access further the meaning-making components of the material they encounter and they switch off from it, claiming perhaps to be 'bored'. They have to be given a sense from the very earliest stage that materials are worth interrogating, indeed it is in our interests to do so, and then they have to be in a position to reach for an available, full armoury of analytical tools.

Contexts

All language discourses are capable of a range of interpretations or 'readings', depending on all the possible situations which might govern them. The same set of words can sound utterly different, even contradictory, expressed in particular ways – or even perceived in a completely different manner from the original intention because the mood or previous actions of the receivers have predisposed them in a particular fashion. How many formerly comic events become distinctly unfunny when set against a tragic background? All directors of Shakespeare understand how context can change everything!

Equally important is the realisation that many language discourses take place in settings and situations which are unfamiliar to some of the participants on occasions; these people should not feel disempowered, intimidated, frightened or overwhelmed in such circumstances.

Creating the identity of individuals

We are our language. The ways in which we think of, understand, assimilate and articulate what we know are through the language we have made part of ourselves. Wittgenstein wrote, 'The limits of my language are the limits of my world.' The challenge for teachers of all children is to discover how much wider the world can become for them, by encouraging the deepest exploration and most confident use of the language available to them; perhaps even discovering new worlds! The problem becomes more acute with the able language user. Sometimes those pupils could be exploring experiences unknown to the teacher, such as young people reading books not familiar to the adult, but that should not deter the teacher from assisting the pupil to make yet further progress.

Aesthetic and metaphoric ideas

Most language study in the last thirty years has been undertaken within the wider context of insight and understanding of 'literature' texts. Much of the energy of

English departments has been devoted to producing young people with the skills of literary critical analysis, able to examine the works of eminent authors, poets and playwrights closely, in a well-understood liberal-humanist tradition supervised by English teachers who have achieved enormous pleasure and fulfilment from their own studies in the subject. There is an accepted, but in many respects limited, progression in the acquisition of these skills, beginning with shared reading comprehension in Key Stage 3, which culminates in the best students studying literature at A level, prior to reading the subject at university.

During the last decade, teachers of English have planned a more balanced approach to textual study, in which non-fiction and media works have been regarded as being as worthy of study as those which are classified as 'great' or 'classical' literature. These alternative texts do not become regarded through this study as being equivalent 'in value' to those texts which have been accepted into the canon of the best of our literature (a list, in itself, not without problems!). Some contemporary educators and commentators, such as Melanie Phillips in *The Observer*, 1.6.97, (*Q*. Who teaches the teachers? *A*. People who think that notices telling you not to do things are as important as Shakespeare), have made the mistake of believing that schools are intent on denigrating the reputation of the works the National Curriculum English orders label: 'major works of literature from the English literary heritage in previous centuries'. (HMSO, 1995)

The reason for this wide-scale misunderstanding can be explained. Schools have very little time in which to study anything, yet out in the world are countless sorts of texts which they know their pupils encounter. It is therefore vital that schools establish clear priorities about what they will include in their language curriculum. If *The Simpsons*, *EastEnders* or *Just Seventeen* are being given classroom attention, so the thinking by some people goes, there is less time for *Hamlet*. What Melanie Phillips and those of like mind fail to acknowledge is the dilemma faced by schools. They have to ask themselves whether it is more beneficial to study the nature of texts and the way they carry and convey meaning, or whether attention should be given to a small, selected group of texts, illustrating what a few important authors (but, of course, not all) have achieved, in the hope that students will apply what they have then learned to other authors. Increasing numbers of English teachers and teacher educators have decided that it is *the nature of texts* which is the more fundamental and empowering aim of their work.

For many students literature represents an alien textual field. The way it is used means that it works as a kind of cultural filter sifting attitudes and responses – advocating some, encouraging others, dismissing these, excluding most and prohibiting still others. Literature represents the textual tastes of some but not others, probably not most – and so many students stand disadvantaged culturally in the face of *Sumitra's Story* as much as in the face of *Great Expectations* or *Henry V*. Those, perhaps who stand to gain from the education system's filtering processes are likely to feel its intrinsic merit. Others may be positioned to experience their indifference to Literature as a lack, a personal and cultural deficit. For me it is the inadequacy of the category of literature that demands the production of new ways of dealing with texts. (Peim, 1995)

Part of this study has included illustrating that *all* texts are constructed (they do not miraculously arrive on classroom desks, unmediated, as some children believe), they reflect the culture, ideas and nuances of their times and contain levels of meanings (not one directed meaning, according to the teacher), capable of being unravelled by pupils who have been taught ways of interrogating texts. Ironically, the nature of this form of study has meant the increasing need for pupils to be knowledgeable about the language of texts, the ways in which the meaning is conveyed: the 'grammar' mastery so sought after, as the grail of improved literacy standards, according to one political faction for the past thirty years.

Yet despite this growing change of attitude, English teachers and class teachers in primary schools realise that they are selling children short if they do not offer a proper proportion of time to the exploration of literature. This study particularly applies to poetry and the nature of narrative, which have such important links with and give insight into so many aspects of our lives. Metaphor is a means through which we rediscover language and push back its known edges. The writers we think of as 'great' have changed the ways we perceive our experiences, enriched the whole language through their creativity and continually helped us to recognise what it is to be fully human: they deserve a substantial amount of curriculum time for those triumphs alone!

The relationship between language, thinking and learning

The Russian psychologist, Vygotsky, has pointed so strongly to the relationship of language and learning, making it clear that learning is not merely brought about by the transmission of information from one person to another.

> Rather, successful teaching is constituted in certain styles of co-operation and negotiation. The importance of this view is that learning depends more on the teacher's dialogue with individuals and groups than on the transfer of information in the form of 'true' statements made by the teacher and remembered by the pupils. (Webster, Beveridge and Reed, 1996)

Vygotsky also has much to suggest to those who have responsibility for the teaching of more able language users, within his theory of a 'zone of proximal development'. This 'zone' is the gap between what children can accomplish on their own and what they might be able to achieve with carefully planned adult help, through the process of 'scaffolding' (careful structuring and support to achieve the next level). Expectations of what children might be capable of achieving with this form of support should be challengingly high.

The pupil as a language learner

When teachers have agreed a set of guiding principles, such as those outlined above, it is much easier for them to plan programmes of work which outline directions of progress their pupils are expected to follow. If, for instance, the school subscribes to the clear intent of ensuring the greatest empowerment of the pupils, it will be seeking the widest range of texts to study and to write in the style of, from the pupils' earliest days in full-time education. Such a school will also be determined to bring about a situation in which pupils are expected to take greater control of their linguistic encounters, where dialogue and negotiation – between teacher and pupils, and pupil and pupil – characterise the learning ethos. Teachers in that setting will not describe a pupil's achievement simply in terms of being, for instance, 'a good writer'. Instead, they should be able to comment more fully on the pupil as a writer of particular types of text, for various reasons to do with the knowledge the child has displayed of the appropriacy, correct form and the effect on the audience of the chosen style of written work. Discussing these important details of their progress with pupils will, in turn, lead to more focused evaluation of the extent of their learning.

In the schools and departments which approach language tasks through these means, pupils will be in a better position to display their skills and knowledge of the texts they read in more searching and wide-ranging ways. Currently, teachers very regularly employ limited strategies to make judgments on their pupils' reading skills. The increased commitment to developing ways of making meaning in relation to a broader reading programme should, in turn, lead to the description of how pupils are progressing on a much wider front.

Much more important will be the ways the pupils themselves should be enabled to reflect on and ask questions of their own learning. If the only feedback a pupil receives of written work is of the 'good work, but mind your spelling', 'not always interesting', 'a much better try' variety (all authentic) then that young person, quite reasonably, is unlikely to be very willing to improve. What help is given for the direction of improvement in such circumstances? If, however, the pupil is pointed to particular spelling problems, or is helped to see that attempts at certain sorts of structuring are inappropriate for reasons which he or she understands, then these could be grounds for improving on the next occasion when written work is attempted. Similar involvement in the ways reading can be improved should be brought about by more explicit explanation and the devising of targets.

The able language user in this setting

A few secondary English departments in Oxfordshire were beginning, during the last few years, to look more closely at the different stages of writing development. Sylvia Karavis and the PAGE team were also exploring, with interested primary schools, just what the characteristics of different types of text might be, and how this knowledge might become areas of teaching to make those features clear to the pupils. An example of this sort of work is given in Figure 4.3. The English teachers involved in this form of study have realised that they have to be far more precise in the ways they are expecting their pupils to improve. Many of them have also recognised that they have some pupils capable of impressive writing and of reading their way through a large number of taxing texts, for whom they have no really developed forms of challenge. Only by identifying the stages of learning in language and literacy will it be possible to place and trace accurately the development of all pupils, including the more able.

Type	Definition	Form	Examples	Features of language at this stage	Teaching necessary	Indicators/signs of development
Recount	a series of happenings, chronologically organised, describing a specific event	diary, journal account, picture, letter	• a visit • an experiment	• past tense, time marked with 'and', 'then' and 'when' • subject of the verb is usually the participants e.g. 'we', 'The horses'	• sequencing events • ordering • discussion of over-use of 'and', and 'then' • emphasise clarity of meaning	• ordered events • greater use of sentence connectives • use of pronouns to avoid repetition
Story/ narrative	set in time, usually contains: opening, characters, actions, events, complication, resolution	wall stories, group stories, picture stories, own books – taped, written, word-processed	• fairy stories • personal narratives • adventure stories • own versions of familiar stories • changed endings of familiar stories	• usually written in the past tense, with an opening, characters, and one or more events, a problem and a resolution	• discuss story structure through reading • tell stories, removing complication, changing endings etc. • discuss feelings and motives of characters • predict endings, change outcomes • discuss layout, speech marks, question marks	• awareness of reader • character development • building up of action • co-ordinating sentences • relative and other subordinate clauses, e.g. the man, whose horse had run away, was left alone
Information	classifying, descriptive or informative, writing about things in general	reference material, fact cards, expert books	• festivals of light • creatures of the night • birds of prey	• usually written in present tense • organised in sections under sub-headings or paragraphs with an introductory statement	• whole class/group discussion of collection of data/facts; ways of organising facts • modelling • organisation of sub-headings etc. • opening statement – what to include? • pairs or groups write one or more sections with support • read aloud from information books	• organisation of information • expanded noun phrases e.g. 'sharp, hooked beak' • use of description

Figure 4.3 Writing – KS1

Produced by P.A.G.E. (Primary Advisory Group for English, Oxfordshire) with Lynne Stephens, Deddington C.E. School, Oxfordshire

Chapter 5

How to Challenge and Improve the Reading of More Able Readers

Key Stage 1

Schools are busy and demanding places, so teachers have too few opportunities to monitor the progress of all aspects of their pupils' academic growth. Yet of all the priorities teachers ought to establish in the first stages of education, probably the most important area of monitoring should be the reading programmes of all the children in their classes. It is essential that somebody in the school keeps an accurate record of the sorts of text being read by the children, of whatever ability.

The real needs of more able readers are too often overlooked or neglected in the reception or infant classroom. As long as these pupils continue to choose and read books, seem to be deriving pleasure from their reading and can manage independently, they attract relatively less attention than their more demanding classmates. This is a most short-sighted position for schools to adopt. Only by genuinely knowing the repertoire of each individual is it possible for the teacher to trace whether real progress has been made, and even the most able should be seen to be improving.

Advisory teacher colleagues in Oxfordshire LEA (PAGE – the Primary Advisory Group for English) published a list of features which define a reader (Figure 5.1). Teachers of young, able readers should be planning activities for their pupils which could lead to improvement across a whole range of criteria included in that list. If the teaching of reading for able readers from the Reception Year to Year 3 is based on that list alone, a child would be making significant progress.

What follows are a number of suggestions, based on the sorts of listed criteria used to define a reader which ought to be employed in classrooms to challenge and support the more able reader, through all phases of the school. It is not essential to insist that the books able readers choose are incrementally more difficult; what matters far more is that the child encounters a full range of texts over time, from which he (or she) derives increasingly deeper insights. I know of able readers in their early teens who read enormously contrasting material in the space of a week, but who still continue to make excellent progress. One 13-year-

Definition of a reader

Interest and motivation
A reader:
- chooses to read and understands that reading is worthwhile
- sometimes wants to share and discuss what has been read
- actively responds to what is read
- loves books and turns readily to a book

Knowledge and expertise
A reader:
- deciphers print for a purpose, e.g. enjoyment, information, and expresses ideas and opinions
- understands that print carries meaning
- can construct meaning from print in the environment
- makes sense of print by drawing on various strategies
- understands the meaning of the text without decoding each word
- understands how stories work
- can, and wants to, predict possible outcomes
- is somebody who reads on the lines, between the lines and beyond the lines
- identifies with what is read and relates what is read to own experience
- draws on previous experience and can predict the possible outcomes
- uses books to make sense of own experience
- looks beyond the literal
- brings prior knowledge/experience to the text and can criticise it
- knows that reading can be a solitary or a social activity
- understands that books can be shared
- can select independently and with confidence
- has the confidence to reject books
- can move into different worlds
- is somebody who reads widely and reads a range of texts and material
- has had experience of language in other contexts, e.g. spoken, story-telling, reading, TV, tapes
- has knowledge of language, including rhyme, rhythm, stories and pictures
- can select, skim and scan a text

Produced by P.A.G.E. (Primary Advisory Group for English, Oxfordshire)

Figure 5.1

old has just completed *Cat's Eye* by Margaret Atwood and is part-way through *The Remains of the Day* by Kazuo Ishiguro. Yet during the last week she has also read *The Mall* (a Point Horror book), her brother's *Beano*, *Woman's Own*, *Just 17*, *The Radio Times*, an article in *The Guardian* weekend supplement, and poems in her GCSE anthology. Different texts satisfy, challenge and give her pleasure at different times of the week in different contexts. She is maturing successfully as a reader; most importantly, she continues to discuss the several sorts of experience reading affords her and considers carefully the choices of increased difficulty, anticipating what she might take from the reading of each new text.

Talking about books

From well before the time children begin reading, they should all be afforded chances to talk about the texts they encounter. Learning about language is a social enterprise and the necessary metalangue a child requires for textual comprehension, comparison and review will only grow from dialogue (not interrogation) with a more experienced and knowledgeable reader. It is not necessary for that person to be a teacher. Most children will talk about books with parents long before they arrive at school, and should continue to do so for as long as possible. The school might look at ways parents give extra attention to more able offspring. Many children talk with their brothers and sisters about books, just as many talk with friends. These dialogues should be encouraged as often as possible, either through play or in more formal contexts. Most schools employ excellent Learning Support Assistants, who often play a significant part in supporting growing readers, and, as I have regularly seen, they can be most effective in the ways they help more able readers.

Younger able readers will benefit from being allotted talk time with older pupils who have shown a similar aptitude at an equivalent stage, who could well have read similar texts and had more time to develop judgments on them, or had further textual experiences against which to compare. A few schools already deploy all older pupils in a 'buddy' reading support system for their younger age group. Where a culture involving this sort of talk is a natural part of the school's reading curriculum arrangements, the older children will be able to contribute much of value to their younger peers through this form of contact. The adults will also gain greater confidence in discussing the nature of texts with the children.

Time given to talk about books

Whoever is nominated to offer support to more able readers, those children have the right to be given time to articulate their perceptions, insights and opinions, and have them challenged and extended. Any time allocated to talking about their reading is certainly as valuable as, if not more valuable than, hearing them read out loud. Enormous value is attached to the process of hearing children read in too many schools, and by many parents, out of all proportion to its overall benefit. I am not suggesting that children should not read aloud, to a teacher or a supporting fellow-reader. In the early stages of reading it is a most necessary way of finding out how children are progressing and keeping track of the strategies and skills they are drawing on and developing. As readers gain more confidence, they must also be given opportunities to increase their fluency by reading aloud in a number of different contexts, not just to their teachers or Learning Support Assistant to have the new page reached recorded in a 'reading record'.

I do assert, however, that the time allocated to hearing a number of pupils reading in many classrooms could be spent more profitably in activities which teach pupils about the ways of 'interrogating' texts, but do not always require the teacher and pupil in one-to-one contact. If reading is regarded as essentially an activity in which the act of decoding is mastered merely to prove and repeat that decoding in encounters with teachers and more proficient readers, then there will be no place for reflection. Pupils brought up in that reading environment could never make satisfactory progress.

More able readers entering the infant school need a much broader programme of reading-related activities to make the progress of which they are capable. These activities do not require them to show their 'sight reading' skills, but rather to draw their thoughts and insights together, as a way of reflecting on their textual engagements. Teachers can make space for this deliberation to take place during reading lessons, through short, regularly directed conversations. Pupils might be sought out at break time, lunch or after school by their 'mentor' and talked to in an informal manner, although a formal record should be made of the child's responses. It is always necessary to keep a note of the stages of development reached, recommendations for further reading, or other suggested ways of opening up meaning. The child might be asked to form a relationship with another adult in the school, perhaps the headteacher, LSA or informed parent helper, on an occasional but systematic basis, to free the teacher for pupils with other demands. Whoever takes on the responsibility of mentoring such a child, or small group of children, should be keeping a record of far more than merely the titles of books which have been read.

As my statement about language/literacy learning claimed earlier (p.33), one of the central concerns of schools in this respect is to empower the child to 'make meaning'. For schools to achieve this complex exercise successfully all pupils have to be able to realise that they can uncover increasingly more difficult layers of meaning in any text they face. They have to feel that the activity is worthwhile and discover that the search is likely to yield unexpected outcomes which have been worth the bother.

Interest might be shown in, for instance:

- how the child came to choose the book in the first place;
- which features of the text might have attracted the child;

- whether scanning took place to decide what sort of text it might be;
- whether the child is familiar with other texts by the same author;
- the perceived level of difficulty and if the book contained some unknown words or ideas;
- whether the book would be worth recommending to others, and who they might be.

These are not knotty or especially skilled areas of questioning, but they do alert the reader to the many possibilities each text could open out for them. Children questioned in this way will also have the chance to realise that becoming a better reader is not dependent on increasing the number of texts they have successfully completed.

In a school where more than one child in a class has been identified as a more able reader, the potential support situation becomes even more interesting. The relevant children should be allowed time together with the supervising adult, and they will learn that being classified a 'good reader' does not mean that they all perceive texts in the same ways. They will quickly realise that they have different interests, might choose their texts for quite diverse reasons and that even their reading strategies are dissimilar. This learning will be far stronger where children are encouraged to work alongside and discuss with older pupils, with whom they can also share these reflections.

There are now considerable numbers of books and articles recommending how to conduct reading interviews, including the very important *Booktalk* by Aidan Chambers. An essay, 'Teaching Children's Literature', in that book summarises what can be gained by talking together about texts, 'not an act of Socratic cross-examination but of participatory conversation, of exploring and sharing; a creative act, mutually enriching.' (Chambers, 1985). The purpose is to expose the possible interpretations of the book.

> Principally what we need to develop is the place of the teacher in a literary discussion. S/he must remain a leader, usually one with a far greater experience of literature than others in the group; but s/he must also behave as just another reader – one among others – all of whom have legitimate and valuable interpretations to offer of any book. As leader, the teacher must help each person discover honestly the book s/he has read; then lead on to discover the book which the author, judged by the narrative's rhetoric, can be agreed upon to have written. And finally, as a result of their corporate and shared experience, the group reconstructs the book they have all read. Thus, the final act is to become aware of the book that comprises each individual interpretation – even the author's – thereby becoming something greater than all. (Chambers, 1985)

Aidan Chambers is also responsible for an additional effective way of involving the reader in another shared, worthwhile discourse about their reading through the approach outlined in *Tell Me: Children Reading and Talk* (Chambers, 1993). Children respond in their own words and offer interpretations, without too many hints or prompts from the questioner. The responses children make about their reading regularly surprises adults, and they should all be accepted. The associations they make with other texts, such as television programmes, comics or other sources which offer similar experiences, are all fertile ground for further discussion, and should be taken seriously. Readers should also, as part of this wider consideration, be encouraged to **cross reference *within* texts** ('where can you find other ideas like that in the book?'/'where are there pictures which remind you of that idea?' etc.).

The value of picture books in extending reading learning

It is tempting to expect children with precocious reading abilities to be able to read for longer periods of time and to be able to make sense of longer, 'chapter-type' books. Teachers and adults might also have an impression of picture books as being unsuitable for these readers, unable to offer sufficient challenge. This belief could not be further from the truth! Most modern picture books are elaborate texts, containing multiple meanings, often depending on the full extent of those meanings to be understood through recognising the essential relationship between the pictures and the writing. Picture books are not just simple reading material designed for those children in the early stages of learning to read. Older, much more experienced pupils, for instance, can gain enormous pleasure and insight from them, commensurate with their increased abilities, and there is, of course, a thriving trade in graphic texts for adults. Young able readers, certainly, should be reading more difficult texts if they wish, and if they can cope with them without struggling. But to expect them to move on to texts for which they are not properly prepared, or which yield little pleasure, is to make reading a monster instead of a delight. The ultimate pleasure reading is capable of giving should never be forgotten, and if young readers do not discover that thrill for themselves they will never make proper progress.

More interesting than facing 'tough texts', young, able readers from the beginning of their formal schooling, should be encouraged to speculate on **what the text is about**. They should be helped to understand that most texts are capable of *multiple meanings*, and it is unlikely that only one reading can be made. An important stage in reading, or meaning-making, growth is when the responder is able to move beyond merely recounting the content or narrative development of the story to speculating about its possible purposes and intentions. Astute young readers will appreciate that John Burningham's *Grandpa* is a book about memories, loss and the exploration of family relationships across the generations. It is also about fantasy and imagination, and not acting one's age. *Where the Wild Things Are*, Maurice Sendak's classic story, is a complex representation of the inside of the mind of a small, angry child, while also being an adventure odyssey and splendid fantasy. *Not Now Bernard* by David McKee is in some respects like the Sendak text. Young children are fascinated by it because they have direct experience of the transformational powers of its central character, which imaginatively empowers him in a world where he is paid too little attention. *Prince Cinders*, by Babette Cole, is a witty, comic tale, but its fun depends on the reader understanding an inversion of normal gender roles in fairy stories, thus introducing an interesting social issue for further discussion. Good readers know that the book with which they are currently engaged is *about* something, and they should actively be encouraged to come up with as many possible suggestions as the text can reasonably support. Picture books are also excellent vehicles through which to explore with pupils how stories work. The beginning of Anthony Browne's *Bear Hunt*, for example, is:

'One day Bear went for a walk.'
'Two hunters were hunting.'

This scene immediately lends itself to a potential drama, and pupils should be asked to suggest what they think is likely to happen in these circumstances, and then check their theories with the actual development of the tale. They could also trace the movement of the plot of the book through a simple diagram, to gain a different perspective of how developments in the text can be traced (see Figure 5.2).

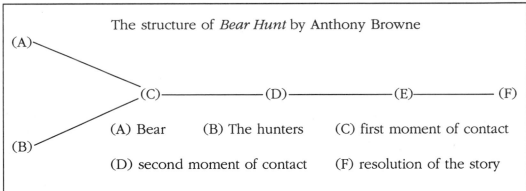

The structure of *Bear Hunt* by Anthony Browne

(A) Bear   (B) The hunters   (C) first moment of contact

(D) second moment of contact   (F) resolution of the story

This structure can be adapted for any story, however complex. More characters would bring about more moments of contact/conflict. (F) is usually easier to predict than moments (C) and (D).

Figure 5.2 Narrative structure of a story

Two popular books by John Burningham, *Oi, Get Off My Train* and *Mr Gumpy's Outing*, are structured in similar cumulative developmental ways, involving animals joining a journey. To have read one of these texts should enable a reader to make accurate predictions about the other. These skills of **prediction** should be a natural feature of the approach to any story, and good readers cannot learn them early enough, but it will be necessary for them to be taught these actual skills in the first place.

Teaching reading to those children who can already read

Learning about reading never stops, even for the most sophisticated reader. Having overcome the hurdle of turning symbols into words which can be easily assimilated into a meaning-making activity, all readers should then be made aware that they have only just begun their journey into texts. Fledgling readers should be helped to notice the differences between different sorts of text, through directed discussion, as soon as possible. More able readers should be able to enjoy this activity from an early stage. To become more accomplished in this skill they will require help in the naming of different **genres** or **forms** they are likely to encounter. Four and five-year-old children will soon begin recognising the important distinguishing features of fiction and non-fiction texts. They should be able to tell the difference between, for instance, *adventure* stories, *family* stories and those involving, perhaps, *animals*. They will not take long to realise that a text such as Jill Murphy's *All in One Piece* is an adventure, involving a family of elephants! The problem with genres is that they are not exclusive, they overlap and their definitions are fluid. They occasionally fail to live up to the, necessarily, very generalised expectations we may have of them. These problems should be regarded as offering even greater areas of interest in textual study.

Yet another area for investigation and discussion could be an **author study**. A child who has read a particularly notable or enjoyable text is likely to look out for other titles by the same author. Readers should be helped to interrogate all the texts they can find written by that author, to discover if there are obvious characteristics which make that writer's works easily recognisable. This sort of study applies just as much to illustrators as authors. Many children choose the texts they wish to read because they enjoy the illustrations as much as the words! Quentin Blake and John Burningham employ their own very recognisable styles of illustration, and children might be challenged to articulate what they see in the drawings of particular artists. Anthony Browne's work owes much to the artist Magritte, and the sometimes dark, often surrealistic nature of his pictures adds considerably to the further meanings of his books. For the child also to know something of the work of Magritte is to add yet another layer of meaning to the textual interpretation. An able child, familiar with this source, could be asked to 'deconstruct' Browne's illustrations for further meaning. Good readers in the early years could also be asked to reflect on the relationship of author and illustrator, and what might be the advantages, or otherwise, of combining both tasks.

A few picture texts contain no words at all, but employ pictures in a narrative sequence, the details to be filled in by readers for themselves. These are also useful teaching tools. Pupils who are already aware of the ways stories are told and unfold should be encouraged to apply their knowledge in these contexts. They could try 'telling the story' in different ways. To realise that it is possible to use the same set of illustrations as the basis for the construction of a range of narratives is a valuable lesson and a further important stage of reading development. Texts such as Raymond Briggs' famous *The Snowman*, Shirley Hughes' *Up and Up*, Jan

Ormerod's *Moonlight* and the beautifully composed collages of *Window* by Jeannie Baker are good examples, which children will enjoy reworking in their own ways.

More confident readers could be asked to supply speech bubbles for the different characters featured in these texts. They should then be asked to replace the bubbles with alternative words, or think of a range of ways in which the words they have ascribed could be spoken. Through this device they can learn how the same pictures are capable of being interpreted in completely different ways.

The very nature of narrative itself can be material for reading study with young children. One area of literary experience they are already likely to know with real confidence is the realm of the fairy tale. The background information they bring would serve them well in a reading of texts such as *Prince Cinders* by Babette Cole, which turns the gender-related problems of the Cinderella story on their head, or *Snow White in New York* by Fiona French, where the Snow White story is given a wonderfully rich, American art-deco setting which evocatively takes it into an almost sleazy, corrupt setting. It would be natural to initiate discussion with able readers on the knowledge they brought to these texts, and how the authors have changed the accepted conventions of these stories. Slightly more demanding, and perhaps for older readers, but very similar in the sorts of reading demands on which it depends, is Jon Scieszka's (with Lane Smith's very characteristic illustrations) *The Stinky Cheese Man and other Fairly Stupid Tales*. Adults often find the style of this book difficult: children love it, especially for the irreverence shown to the well-known tales in our language.

Other comparative study might be encouraged around repeated or similar themes or ideas in picture books. In John Burningham's *Mr Gumpy's Outing* are the lines:

'May I come, please, Mr Gumpy?' said the pig.
'Very well, but don't muck about.'

'Have you a place for me?' said the sheep.
'Yes, but don't keep bleating.'

which children enjoy, because they recognise the stereotype is establishing the character. In Joy Cowley's *The Little Yellow Chicken* are the following lines, used in very much the same way:

'Hop it!' said the frog.
'Buzz off!' said the bee.
And the big brown beetle said, 'Stop bugging me!'

As well as the fun children have in recognising the humour in those lines, they will also become better attuned to reading other narratives where such devices are employed.

The contents of a book are, rightly, the first concerns of readers and teachers, but books should also be regarded as 'packages', and the reader should be aware of all the parts which contribute to the final product. Books, after all, are media products – no more, no less – like all other media products. They are constructed products, involving the decision-making and cooperation of large numbers of people. They do not arrive, as some children seem to think, fully formed, neutral and somehow 'pure', untouched by the world! This greater knowledge will contribute to any child's repertoire of textual choice; yet another area of empowerment.

Books might be in paperback covers, hardback covers, or, in the case for the very young, rag covers. It is worth considering why. The covers are invariably illustrated, usually with a picture selected from the contents. 'Why that picture, rather than others?', is a reasonable question. There might be different editions of the same text title available, which could have different covers, giving rise to further discussion. The name of the author and the title of the book appear a number of times, possibly in different typefaces, and the publisher's decisions about those are worth considering. Is there an ISBN? What is it? What is the publisher's name? Are there other books in the classroom, the library, that the child owns, which have been published for young children by that publisher? Is it possible to recognise a particular publisher's texts by clear characteristics? The blurb begins to frame a reader's expectations about the likely contents of the book: what sort of anticipatory feelings does that child bring to the reading? Are there references to other texts – books, television programmes, videos? All these questions lead to the reader knowing more about reading, why people read, and how choices about books are made and mediated.

Knowledge about the places where children are likely to have access to books are also helpful to young readers. They could look at the ways books are stored in school, whether in the classroom, the library or both, and be involved in rearranging the books in different genre 'packages'. If the children belong to public libraries they could also explore how the library is physically divided, and where the books on topics in which they are interested are situated. What sorts of extra attention does the library pay to younger readers? Where are the information books stored in relation to the fiction texts? Children with advanced reading skills could draw up their own questions on these topics. They could also be asked to think about a similar investigation in relation to book shops.

All these insights and ways of 'knowing' about texts are important components contributing to children's ability to *reflect* on their own progress as readers; the ultimate goal of self-knowledge about their learning which every child should be assisted in attaining. To be thought of as 'good' readers children should be able to articulate what is looked for in texts, where and when reading is enjoyed, what has proved particularly challenging, what sorts of targets have been set, whose recommendations they trust most, amongst other topics. Answers to these questions empower children to decide 'where next?' in their reading growth.

Commercial reading schemes and the reader

In Chapter 2 I referred to children who have been unnecessarily delayed in their reading development by being made to pass through some or all of the stages of a commercial reading scheme. I do not intend a blanket disapproval of these schemes, or of any other resource which has the possibility of supporting reading growth, particularly when teachers are aware of which aspects of the scheme they are using, for which clear purposes. It should be obvious from all the suggestions which I have made in this chapter so far, however, that there are huge areas of reading knowledge which can be used to conduct real dialogue between the child and the more experienced reader. When considering scheme books the following question should be asked:

- Do the books have identifiable authors?
- Are the texts of those authors possible to identify from shared qualities?
- Is the relationship between the words and the illustrations an important element in the fuller meaning making of the whole text?
- Is the language especially devised for teaching purposes, or does it mirror rhythms and patterns of real language interaction?
- Are the texts about something?
- Are the contents of the texts concerned with areas of experience to which the children can relate?
- Do characters and settings in the texts reflect areas of the readers' own lives?

If the answers to these questions are mostly negative, or the books do not lend themselves to this form of interrogation, the final question has to be, 'are the texts really offering worthwhile support and challenge to any class of reader?' They will certainly not be asking much of children already showing significant accomplishment.

Reading poetry with young able readers

Much of the poetry these children will already have encountered will be in the form of nursery rhyme and song. Relations with these forms will be continued when the child arrives at school, but more specific attention might be given to the rhymes children sing, to ensure that they are aware they are engaging with a piece of verse. Too much poetry is transparent and children are not aware that they are in its presence! To empower those young pupils who think a little more intensely about language and its use to look out for the contrast between the metaphoric and the literal is to engender a life-long skill.

Just as more able readers should be directed towards particular forms of non-fiction, so they can also be helped to include poetry on their reading lists. In one school where these children were identified, I have seen a Learning Support Assistant working with children in separate age groups. With each group she had found a number of appropriate poems on the subject of water, and was reading the poems with them and beginning the process of informal poetic analysis, building from simple meaning-making procedures. The impression of sounds and the sorts of associations the words fostered were discussed. The children were then encouraged to write their own poems, either working within the styles of the poems they had read, or adopting new ones. This is a straightforward and very valuable approach. The important factor is that children keep as balanced a view as possible of the reading repertoire they should maintain.

Children should be immersed in as much poetry as can be found for them. Able language users will usually be delighted to learn by heart new verse they find and it can be a useful skill to develop from entry to school. If poetry retelling can be made into something of a dramatic or presentational event, so much the better, as the child will find how expression, timing and tone can contribute to conveying the full meaning to the listener.

In magazines dealing with primary literacy topics, such as *The Primary English Magazine*, published by Garth Publishing, and *Language & Learning*, published by The Questions Publishing Company, it is possible to find a host of excellent articles promoting poetry familiarisation and learning. John Lynch, in *The Primary English Magazine* (Vol 1, number 2), for instance, provides a report of an after-school poetry club he runs at Handford Hall CP School in Ipswich. An impressive feature of John's approach is the emphasis he places on drafting, and his high expectation of the pupils. He is not prepared to accept first attempts, but manages to give real value to the process of reworking the material, through a feedback process he employs to encourage pupils to think more carefully about their work. Pupils should not be given the impression that merely to create a piece of verse is admirable or sufficient; they have to realise from an early stage that the communication of precise meaning requires asking some tough questions about it. This is often managed through club members reading their poetry aloud to each other. John also places huge value on pairing younger and older pupils together to compose their work: ideal for more able poets!

Other forms of narrative reading

If teachers are teaching reading, they are likely to be holding conversations with pupils about the characteristics of texts, as I have already outlined. Yet the likelihood is that these discussions will mostly be about books, and usually the sorts of books 'validated' by the school. Teachers must also remember that children, of all abilities, actually come into contact with an enormous range of texts, and they require *meaning-making* skills to achieve a full sense of these materials just as much as they need to be able to 'read' books.

Similar sorts of opportunity should be allowed to enable pupils to analyse and discuss these alternative texts: e.g. comics, cartoons, television programmes, video, film, computer games, newspapers. They are, after all, *constructed* texts, just as much as story books (indeed, some texts often derive from the same narratives) and we should be interested in helping these pupils to *deconstruct* all the texts with which they come into contact. The LINC (Language in the National Curriculum) page 'A Framework for Looking at Texts (Figure 4.2, p.35) reminds us that there are common analytical approaches possible to apply to all sorts of text. Even the youngest confident readers should be helped towards applying these methods of analysis. So some points to begin discussion might be:

- What am I 'reading' or watching?
- How do I know what it is?
- What can I already say about this sort of text?
- Do I know how this text is put together?
- What do I find attractive or interesting about this text?
- Do I look out for this sort of text, or did I come across it by chance?
- In what settings do I best enjoy this text?
- When am I most likely to come across this sort of text?
- Are there things about this text I recognise in other forms of text?

Reading non-narrative texts

Most children learn to read with fiction, narrative-based materials and they comprise a large portion of the reading diet of all children during their first years in school. There is an assumption by most people that a child able to read fiction texts will also be able to read non-fiction as proficiently. The work of Alison Littlefair (*Reading All Types of Writing*, OUP, 1991), Bobbie Neate (*Finding Out About Finding Out*, Hodder and Stoughton, 1992) and Dee Reid and Diana Bentley (*Reading On!*, Scholastic, 1996) makes clear how different the demands of reading non-fiction can be from those of fiction, and how teachers must be prepared to help pupils in their meaning-making activities in this often unfamiliar linguistic territory. The table in Figure 5.3 points to a simple comparison between fiction and non-fiction texts, and highlights the necessity of properly preparing children for effective reading of information and reference texts. Good readers are too often expected to cope for themselves in the context of research and project work, in the mistaken belief that they are capable of finding their way through any materials. They really do need focused support.

The text books of different subjects are usually written in particular ways and the successful learning of non-fiction reading will depend on the child's ability to discern the whole range. Young children are capable of recognising different *types of text*, and they can be shown how different types are used for specific purposes. A Reception/Year 1 class in a city school had been made familiar with the simple convention of *procedural writing* (the writing of instruction, procedures or initiation of action, found in mathematics texts, recipes and MFI or IKEA home furniture construction!). They discovered through carefully structured exploration

Language of fiction	Language of non-fiction
Whole text	
– Personal	– Impersonal
– Characters/agents who propel the action forward	– Impersonal and passive construction
– Generally chronological therefore reader is impelled through the text	– Non-chronological, decontextualised
– Language is narrative, and frequently contains dialogue	– Language is less cohesive and rarely contains dialogue
– Few different nouns, more pronouns	– Large number of new nouns and verbs. Fewer pronouns
– Becomes progressively easier to read as plot and character develop	– Can become more difficult to understand as reader has to absorb increasing amounts of information. The reader frequently needs to stop, to refer back, to re-read
– Meaning is organised through familiar linguistic signposts – chapters and recognisable time markers, e.g. *Once, long ago, the next day*	– Meaning is organised through different linguistic signposts, e.g. *moreover, therefore*. The reader needs to know that these signal additional information

Figure 5.3 The language of fiction and non-fiction

that the verbs in this type of writing are mostly commands or imperatives – 'mix', 'sieve', 'chop' – and they knew that writing their recipes for cooking lessons had to be composed in this style. The appropriateness of particular types of writing is a topic that cannot be taught too soon; better readers should be directed towards developing their knowledge of these processes as soon as possible. Teachers should be planning activities which allow pupils to explore and draw their own conclusions about text types and how they are applied in different contexts.

Sometimes, publishers of information texts, particularly those for the youngest readers, have trouble deciding on exactly which type of text they are employing. It is not unusual for an information book about, for instance, 'Water' to begin: 'It's raining. On go our raincoats and up go our umbrellas!' Young, able readers need to be able to recognise that such texts move in and out of a narrative style, in sometimes quite confusing ways. They should be assisted in the process of recognising the factual material which is relevant for their learning purposes.

Organising reading activities for the more able

The best classroom provision for more able readers always depends on the numbers of such children in that particular class. One child with advanced skills can cause problems in a class of twenty five or more, where most children are attempting to acquire basic literacy skills, and the best support might well have to be given through occasional conversations with a 'reading mentor' (the class teacher, a special needs teacher, the headteacher, learning support assistant or delegated, informed parent helper), to check on progress. Two or more such children in a class will allow teachers to plan collaborative exploration of texts, with the increased possibility of children learning from each other. If three, four or more children are thought to be more able, then supported group work can begin from the earliest days, to everybody's benefit if organised carefully.

The shared study of texts provides an excellent vehicle for establishing routines in the approach to reading for the more able, reinforcing the sorts of questions children should be applying to their textual encounters. The members of the group will also hear which features of a text play a part in the choices and preferences of others, and share with them their rereadings. They are also likely to broaden their knowledge of texts, by hearing of titles, stories and situations they would otherwise not have have discovered for themselves.

Information from sources other than books

Teachers are aware that children increasingly draw their knowledge of the world from a widening variety of sources, of which books are playing a relatively smaller part. The use of encyclopaedias and other reference texts now available on computers, CD-roms and the internet means that children have to call on a wider repertoire of meaning-making, information-seeking skills. Not only do they need to be able to read the information on screen, just as they might with a book, they also – possibly more importantly – have to select, from often large areas of text, the actual information they seek. The necessity of being familiar with an **index** and **lists of contents** and using the skill of **cross-referencing** in these circumstances is obvious.

The relationship between reading and writing

The relationship between reading and writing must be constantly re-emphasised for more able language users. Pupils should be continually encouraged to read for the purposes of developing and improving their writing as well as for the knowledge they will acquire and the pleasure they will derive. To increase their writing fluency and confidence their attention should be drawn to the simplest of grammatical structures. Examples of the sorts of exploration they could be conducting might include counting the number of words in a sentence in a story text, compared with the number of words in a sentence in an information text. They could explore the number of clauses in sentences in the two sorts of writing, or consider how often nouns appear in both – and which sorts. It would be difficult to conduct this work without actually referring to some of the names of parts of speech, but this does not mean indulging in decontextualised 'grammar' exercises. Quite the contrary. These children can easily recognise and begin to think about the function of nouns and verbs, and in Key Stage 1 that will be a sound enough foundation.

Key Stage 2

The initial stages of reading are usually taught well in infant schools, but the follow-up which should sustain and promote further reading attainment is not always so well-understood by teachers in junior schools. This state of affairs applies just as much to more able readers as it does for those in the mainstream. All readers require a broader repertoire of reading skills to meet the more demanding curriculum requirements of Key Stage 2, but more able readers have to be challenged against their own skills too. It has been too easy for able readers, particularly boys, to fall back at this stage and fail to reach their potential.

Much of the teaching that is necessary to promote the strongest reading interest and development at this stage of schooling resembles that which should have characterised good procedure in Key Stage 1. **Reading reflection** remains the important centre of attention and pupils should be encouraged to think broadly about their reading practices, preferences and proficiency. At all Key Stages it should be a point of learning principle that pupils can only gain real benefit from the reflective process if they have been fully apprised of just what it is they are supposed to be doing. It is not enough to plan a 'reading' lesson or session, without focusing on an area where pupils are able to ask themselves if they have improved through taking part in that activity. If no discernible progress has taken place teachers should consider what has impeded it, or which problems need extra attention before that new ground can be reached.

At this stage pupils should be expected to keep records of their progress in a variety of ways; not just in the form of reading reviews. It is worth bearing in mind that some readers, asked to write too often about the many texts they read, regard this sort of follow-up activity, if imposed too often, as a punishment. A few pupils have been known to slow down in their reading because they believe that they are going to be 'punished' by having to write yet another review as a consequence! The record keeping for able readers can offer creative challenges to teachers and pupils. It might be a reasonable compromise during the junior years for the fast reading, confident child, who is capable of drawing extensive meaning from a wide variety of texts, to keep an overall mechanical record of titles of texts read, and names of authors and publishers, only writing reviews of occasional agreed selected texts. The reviews themselves could then become the focus of progression in reading, by requiring the child to emphasise different and more complex aspects of the texts read over time. Increasing the difficulty of the task could include more comparison of texts, basing reviews on more demanding review 'models' or examples, or the expectation of less narrative content and more assessment of particular features.

Reading fiction in Key Stage 2

The best readers will probably already have begun reading books divided into chapters and composed in smaller type than that of picture books. As a matter of course they should be employing **prediction** activities after having read the first few paragraphs, and they should regularly get into the habit of suggesting in which **genre(s)** the book might have been written. All these preliminaries will be helpful in assisting the meaning-making so necessary for the most comprehensive understanding of texts.

Even good readers will require assistance in exploring the many different genres available, either through recommendations of the teachers, or through a relationship with other knowledgeable adults, such as a local librarian or staff of the local schools' library service, where that service still exists. Schools should themselves keep as up to date as possible about the publication of new fiction, available through such sources as *Books for Keeps*, or the review pages of the *TES*, or the education and children's sections of newspapers such as *The Guardian* and *The Independent*. These different publications will also, from time to time, publish lists of the titles of books nominated for the major awards: The Carnegie Medal; *The Guardian* Children's Fiction Award; Smarties Book Prize, amongst other distinguished honours. The Young Book Trust also lists these prizewinners, going back over some years, as well as publishing *100 Best Books*, 'the pick of paperback stories for children from toddlers to teenagers', each year.

A very real exercise to undertake with all children, but especially important for more able readers, is to buy copies of all five or six novels on a nominated short list for a literary prize, ask the children to read them and decide their own winner. The best readers could be expected to read them all (it might be necessary to delay the announcement of the actual award-winner, to allow time for this exercise to take place), and compare their choices with those of the professional judges. The enormous value of a project such as this can be gauged in a number of ways. It will ensure that the school keeps up with contemporary trends and titles, it demands that the best pupils engage in a real-life reading activity, it underlines the need to make clear and substantial judgments which can be intelligently and persuasively made to others, and it illustrates just how fragile and subjective human choices can be – even when made by adults!

Reading of fiction in Key Stage 2 has to be carefully directed and lead to continued growth for all readers. More able textual interrogators should be given every chance to show their significantly enhanced skills, and display so many pronounced abilities that the receiving secondary school English departments *have* to take notice of them and make proper provision at the time of transfer. Teachers should be able to describe to a parent who is asking direct questions about reading growth, through which areas of reading the able child has made real advancement, with more supporting detail than the mere listing of texts covered.

Pupils with pronounced talent should, at this stage, be able to call on a broad systematic checklist of questions they put to themselves when working through a fiction text. The questions could be printed for individuals to apply for themselves, or become a shared task for a group. They might include topics like:

1. **Author** Have you read other works by this author?
   - Is this text like the other work(s) you have read?
   - Are there any differences between this text and others by this author?
   - Is this text like any others you know by other authors?
2. **Characters** Who are the main characters in the text?
   - Are all the important characters encountered in the early part of the text?
   - What do I learn about them which contributes to my understanding later in the story?
   - Do the characters change?
   - Are the characters like people I know?
   - Do the characters represent certain things/ideas?
3. **Settings** What do I learn about the setting?
   - Is there more than one setting?
   - Will the setting(s) play a vital part in the rest of the story?
   - Are there particular features of the setting(s) which are made important?
4. **Narrative voice** Who tells the story?
   - Is the story told by more than one story teller?
   - Does my view of the narrative depend on this person's telling?
   - Why do I think the author has selected this voice/these voices?

Beyond this group of questions, however, are other considerations which the more able readers could be applying each time they read a new text, in the classroom context and at home, if they are prepared to do so. I would not wish to suggest that every book which is read should be subjected to this catechism, but once a reader has begun to work in this manner these considerations will be more naturally applied. Further areas of study might be:

5. **Genre** In which genre(s) do I place this text?
   - Does it more strongly lean towards one particular genre, or is it a mixture of genres?

- Which features of the genre(s) did I recognise?
- Have I read other texts which resembled this genre?
6. **Narrative** Did the narrative proceed as I expected?
   - Were there twists or developments which surprised me?
   - At which points of the narrative did significant events take place?
   - Did I find the narrative convincing? Was it meant to be?
7. **Language** Did I find the language easy to read through the whole text?
   - Were there some parts more difficult than others?
   - What was unusual about the difficult parts?
   - Did I think that the difficult parts were interesting and worth continuing with?
   - Are there some sections which are really important to the central meaning of the text?

Just as with Key Stage 1 readers, it is not necessary to expect these older pupils to illustrate their advanced reading abilities by tackling very long or deliberately difficult texts. Real progression in the reading of fiction is marked by being able to ask independently the sorts of questions shown above, of any sort of text, and by making increasingly detailed responses which expose further layers of meaning. It is better for a child to be able to make full sense of Philip Pullman's *The Firework Maker's Daughter* or Terry Pratchett's *Truckers* in a comfortable way than to wade unhappily through Dickens' *Great Expectations* simply because it is regarded as a 'great text'. By that statement I do not mean that any one of those texts is more worthwhile than any other, I merely reiterate that classical texts from a previous age do not, simply by their reputations, become superior and bestow extra reading powers on those who find their way through them.

Studying classic texts

This is also an excellent place to state that it is essential for young readers to have had experience of important children's texts from the past two centuries, or from further back in time. In the same way that children will miss important references in our shared culture, even our popular culture, if they are not acquainted with *The Bible* and the works of Shakespeare, so they should have opportunities to discover what has moved, excited and interested others of their age for many years. Therefore, *The Wind in the Willows, Alice in Wonderland, The Secret Garden* and *The Water Babies*, to mention only a tiny few in a very long list of such texts, should be part of the reading diet of all pupils, not merely the more able. The National Curriculum expects that all in Key Stage 2 will have read 'some long-established children's fiction' (DfE, 1995), and they add an extra dimension to a well-balanced reading curriculum.

I would like to propose that the study for the more able could focus on their ability to identify the characteristics of the text which make it very obviously of its own time. Some areas of closer scrutiny might be on the ways characters are drawn, the language – particularly the vocabulary – employed in the text, and the sorts of values the text embodies. Young readers will enjoy comparing the background and settings of the stories, especially the stark differences in living standards of the different classes, and the relationships between them. This more demanding approach has always been regarded as the preserve of the secondary school, yet pupils who have already become accustomed to comparative study of two or three texts should be fully prepared to undertake more testing broader comparison of books from different times, even in Key Stage 2. They could also be set the task of considering why these particular stories have become favourites for so long and why publishers still have no difficulty in deciding to print them. Pupils can be helped to see much about attitudes to children's reading over time if they are encouraged to compare the covers, blurbs and illustrations from different editions of these texts, printed at different periods.

Another level of study could concern the attitudes to the heroes and heroines embodied within more traditional, older texts compared with those to be found in contemporary publications. Virtually any edition of *Cinderella* would be suitable for comparison with *Prince Cinders* by Babette Cole, at a number of levels. There are also other texts which would encourage fascinating comparison: *The Paper Bag Princess* by Robert Munsch and Michael Martchenko, *Princess Smartypants* by Babette Cole and *Snow White in New York* by Fiona French would give all readers plenty to talk about when read alongside a classic fairy tale.

My former colleagues in the Oxfordshire PAGE team selected a number of contemporary editions of the same traditional story, in picture book form, for directed comparative study. One example is *Hansel and Gretel*. They chose a Macmillan edition, illustrated by Susan Jeffers, with 'The Brothers Grimm' as named authors; another version, published by Little Mammoth, is illustrated by Anthony Browne with 'The Brothers Grimm' again the acknowledged authors; the third version is told and illustrated by Tony Ross, published by Andersen Press. These texts are so very different, they offer sufficient material for a whole term's reading study!

The covers and blurbs of these three versions are the first points of departure. All feature illustrations of Hansel and Gretel, but represented in utterly different ways. Susan Jeffers has drawn the two children in close up, placed in a wood, but not looking very frightened. There is even a comforting white bird in the background. Anthony Browne shows two small children huddled into the space at the bottom of a tree, their faces sad and forlorn, with a dark wood behind. Tony Ross offers two cartoon children, both clearly upset, standing in a wood, looking off to one side of the cover, while their woodman father, with a powerful axe over his shoulder, looks back regretfully on them from the top right hand side. The image is extremely stark, despite its colour. The blurb of the Susan Jeffers edition emphasises the traditional Grimm background. Anthony Browne's version summarises the plot on the back cover, while the Tony Ross text is clearly a modern retelling, part of a series of similar undertakings with favourite tales.

Even though two of the texts are supposedly by The Brothers Grimm, they are similar in their words, but not exactly the same. The Susan Jeffers version is more traditional, reflecting the 'softer' illustrative style. Anthony Browne's edition, on the other hand, is darker and bleaker, both in the pictures and some of the writing style. Tony Ross is uncompromising in his depiction of the wicked stepmother:

'Take 'em away and dump 'em in the forest,' she told her husband.
'No!' he said. 'I love them.'
'They are two extra, useless, snivelling mouths to feed,' she snarled.

This exciting starting point for more intense language study is one which will quickly engage those children who have a greater facility for the way language works. All readers will enjoy being shown how to explore these differences in the books, but the more able should be taking on similar comparative exercises for themselves. Teachers have to ensure that they have allowed their pupils access to the necessary resources to bring this study about, and then to have set them extension tasks which alert readers to specific areas of difference.

Other textual study

Sometimes pupils, of whatever ability, become 'stuck' for a while on particular authors, whilst their parents and teachers despair about them ever moving on to what are perceived to be more demanding books. I have regularly heard, for instance, of adults worrying about children taking an undue interest in Enid Blyton, Roald Dahl or the Point Horror series. Such detailed knowledge of one author or type of text offers a real teaching opportunity. Pupils should be assisted in exploring the characteristics of these texts which collectively identify them. In Enid Blyton books, what do devoted readers expect of the characters? Are the ways in which these characters are described the same from book to book? How often in the story does exciting activity take place? How is that action described? How are the 'villains' identified, and which aspects of their nature are highlighted? Older readers in Key Stage 2 could be asked to devise their own questions to put to a series such as Goosebumps or Point Horror. Through this device it is possible that some children will come to their own decisions about the limited nature of such continued reading, as I have heard Year 4 pupils actually articulate.

Even if the readers are not 'stuck', this approach can still be employed as a useful teaching device. Series of stories, such as Humphrey Carpenter's *Mr Majeika* and Ann Jungman's *Vlad the Drac*, depend on the readers being familiar with certain details recurring in all the different versions. Vlad, for instance, does not have a happy relationship with Mr Stone, father of the family which features in all the books. Vlad is always a little out of date in his knowledge of events and only enjoys eating soap products! He cannot quite manage to find his way back to Transylvania, despite the encouragement and active help of the family. Listing these identifiable, shared features should be well within the abilities of able readers, developed from similar but less demanding activities of Key Stage 1 pupils.

Teachers could consider encouraging pupils to read a selection of texts linked thematically. For older Key Stage 2 readers a suitable topic would be texts written about the war – from very different perspectives. Judith Kerr's *When Hitler Stole Pink Rabbit* would, for instance, make an excellent companion piece with *Friedrich* by Hans Peter Richter, and possibly *Anne Frank's Diary*. All these texts are concerned with Jewish children directly affected by the build up to, and onset of, war in mainland Europe. Comparison could then be made with *Blitzcat* by Robert Westall, *Goodnight Mr Tom* and *A Little Love Song* by Michelle Magorian, and Nina Bawden's *Carrie's War*, which mostly deal with the impact of the second world war on British young people. Non-fiction texts appropriately associated with this 'project' are: *No Time to Say Goodbye*, Ben Wicks's compilation of memories of evacuees, and Michael Foreman's *War Boy*, an autobiographical account of a boy's experiences in wartime Lowestoft (illustrated with many examples of contemporary non-fiction texts). Reading all or most of these texts might be regarded as a huge demand, but the really challenging part is to be found in making comparisons of experiences, studying the ways those experiences have been narrated and discovering the different areas of focus across the range of titles. The whole study would be much more beneficial to its participants, and its outcomes likely to be better developed and more interesting, if it was structured as a group activity.

Similar studies could be undertaken at any part of the Key Stage, using appropriate texts for the readers concerned. It is possible to construct thematic associations from virtually any source, indicating to pupils that texts can be read from all sorts of different viewpoints. Younger pupils, for instance, could be asked to compare and ask questions of the ways the different animals appearing in *The Frog Prince* by Kaye Umansky, *Charlotte's Web* by E.B. White, *The True Story of the Three Little Pigs* by Jon Scieszka and Lane Smith, *Snowy* by Berlie Doherty and *Badger's Parting Gifts* by Susan Varley are represented. What reactions are we expected to have about these animals? What expectations of the way humans regard animals are we drawing on when making our meanings about these texts? These kinds of questions would occupy an able group in their reading lessons for a reasonable length of time.

As discussed in an earlier section, pupils should be fully aware that books are usually *about* something. Many texts suitable for study by more able Key Stage 2 readers could also be used for wider discussion about important issues which occupy young people of this age. Anne Fine's work is often concerned with important current social issues: *Madame Doubtfire* deals with the effects of divorce on the children; *The Tulip Touch* is a sad, disturbing story of child neglect and abuse leading to tragic consequences; *Bill's New Frock* is an amusing fantasy exploring expectations about gender, while *Flour Babies* examines matters of caring and responsibility for others. Elizabeth Laird's *Red Sky in the Morning* is a moving study of physical handicap and death, which usually has a powerful effect on readers. An uncompromising scrutiny of bullying is at the centre of *The Present Takers* by Aidan Chambers, while Morris Gleitzman's *Two Weeks with the Queen* achieves the almost impossible goal of dealing with the issue of Aids in a tasteful and funny way.

Poetry study

More able language users should be given the strongest possible introduction to poetry, because it is in the language of poetry that many of them will find enormous pleasure and challenge. If children have already shown an inclination to seek for further meaning in what they read, poetry will serve as an area of literature where they can hone and refine those skills. At Key Stage 2 teachers will not have much time available to devote solely to poetry, particularly for one small section of the classroom population, but they should be empowering the more confident language users to read, compare and make meaning for themselves.

A balanced classroom collection of texts or a school library worth revisiting should contain a selection of poetry anthologies in which children are encouraged to browse purposefully. Browsing can so often be interpreted as merely turning pages, in the hope of lighting on something of interest and value. To make this activity more focused, the children should be searching for some particular features: they might be looking for similar subject matter; they might be seeking poems which rhyme; their attention could be pointed towards poems of a particular form — sonnets, ballads, elegies, etc. It is almost impossible to know where to begin with the study of poetry and, in the long run, best to discover what is possible by bringing about an atmosphere where pupils can be immersed in some of its forms. Yet from that immersion the teacher needs to be able to offer specific platforms of knowledge on which pupils can build their own ladder of progression.

Pupils should also be expected to find examples of poetry in their wider lives, beyond the boundaries of its study in school. Advertisements are a constant source of poetic ideas and devices (slogans such as Zanussi's 'The appliance of science' and Fiat's 'Driven with passion' are both good examples). Rap poetry is currently evident in many contexts, and illustrates the sort of fun to be had playing with words, but not many pupils recognise it is a genuine form of poetry. A number of pupils in English schools are born into different cultures, and they should be encouraged to bring to the classroom poetic forms which are important to their lives and illustrate how different peoples use language in different ways. We should also not forget that poetry can be great fun: pupils of all abilities need to be entertained by poetry through acquaintance with language in the forms of jokes, puns, light verse and limericks.

Two Year 5 pupils, a boy and a girl, had been given assistance in their study of the *sonnet*. At first their work was mechanical, based on the recognition of the sonnet form from a number of anthology sources. They discovered some examples of sonnets by Shakespeare, Wordsworth, Shelley, Robert Frost and a few modern poets. They then spent time talking together, merely trying to understand what the poems where about, occasionally becoming very excited about the meanings they discovered. Not surprisingly, they found it easier to work back chronologically from the modern poems, but they slowly became more accomplished readers of the older versions through their increasing confidence. Given some hints about Shakespearian and Petrarchan sonnet forms they delved further into their examples to discover which patterns fitted the instances they had chosen, and tried to ask further questions of the meaning given that knowledge. This sort of approach can offer a better engagement for more able boys, who are often uncomfortable with, or find it difficult to articulate, their feelings about poetry. They enjoy a more systematic base to their study, not just of poetry but most literature they are asked to read.

I have heard of other excellent study of the *ballad* with pupils from different ages within Key Stage 2. Alfred Noyes' *The Highwayman*, especially in the edition illustrated by Charles Keeping (OUP, 1981), and the works of Charles Causley have been seen as examples easily accessible for study by these pupils. Once again, they were asked as a necessary preliminary to make as much sense of the poems as they could in silent and shared readings, then urged to discover the details of characterisation and action conveyed through the language in collaborative closer analysis. One group, working with *The Highwayman*, considered what the poem might have been like as prose and how the poetic form changed the sort of language employed, and the effects it engendered. Another discussed in great detail who they felt to be the most important character in *The Highwayman*. These open-ended approaches allowed the pupils to make enquiries from different angles, which was an important lesson for further literary investigation.

It is not essential, however, to expect this very demanding level of work from more able pupils to ensure that they are engaging with poetry. Teachers can support and challenge by simply ensuring that poetry is being read. They can include questions about poetry in their regular *booktalk* sessions with pupils. Asking the pupils to name current favourite poems and explaining why they enjoy reading them is a helpful beginning to further poetry study. Children should be encouraged to learn favourite poems, or sections of them, and recite them in supportive atmospheres. Having established interest with the pupils, and a realisation on their part that poetry is worth looking into, the teacher should be planning for further progression.

Of course, if children wish to write their own poetry, they should be given every assistance to do so. There are contexts in which poetry writing practice should be planned for all children, which might include activities such as devising similes and metaphors; cutting a piece of prose to the bare bones; recreating experience or learning through verse forms; writing pastiche versions of published poetry. It should not, however, always be an expectation that a finished complete poem will be the final outcome of these exercises. Most poetry is difficult, both to understand at different levels and to write. Children may well have succeeded in their efforts if they convey well the concentrated meaning to be found in just a few lines or fragments of poems; so a few genuine lines of poetic form can be as worthwhile as pages of doggerel, where the meaning has been overridden by the obsession with rhyme. No child will benefit from being told that the poetry is 'good' when it clearly is not, and few will be helped by believing that poetry can be created easily, when it demands enormous attention and reworking – even by published poets!

Non-fiction study

In Key Stage 2 all readers will be using a greater range of information and non-fiction texts from which to acquire knowledge. More able readers will need the same sort of tuition required by all pupils to recognise many of the differences between fiction and non-fiction material, but they could be given more independent, exploratory study through which to make their insights and draw their own conclusions.

There are countless types of texts now being produced in the world, and children are increasingly aware of many of them. The starting point for the study of non-fiction could be in drawing up lists of texts they know about. I worked with two able Year 3 pupils, scrutinising the different available non-fiction texts to be found in their own classroom. We came up with:

> encyclopaedias, information books on general topics (geography), information texts on specific topics (e.g. Dorling Kindersley *Castles*), spelling lists, the register, group lists, National Curriculum documents, assembly materials, books about education, reading records, number charts, labels and captions on pictures, audio cassette inserts, dictionaries, thesauruses, exercise books, information posters, wall displays of a science experiment, 'emergency exit' sign, instructions for the heater, newspapers used to cover tables for art, etc.

It was a genuinely illuminating activity!

Having looked with some care at their own classroom, the pupils should then be asked to list the different sorts of non-fiction texts they might find in many other possible different contexts: the environment directly outside the school, different sorts of shop, the library, the home, being just a few. Between them they should yield an immense list. We need to help pupils make more sense of this enormous profusion of available types of text, and Alison Littlefair in *Reading All Types of Writing* (1991) offers some helpful advice to begin categorising them. She suggests designating non-fiction texts under the following headings:

- *the expository genre:* examples being guide books, text books, newspapers, information leaflets and brochures;

- *the procedural genre:* examples being lists of instructions, guide books, stage directions, recipes, forms;
- *the reference genre:* examples being dictionaries, encyclopaedias, computer data, maps, catalogues.

Using only these sorts of simple headings, it should be possible for children to begin to think about the characteristics which determine into which categories texts should be placed.

Dee Reid and Diana Bentley in *Reading On!* (ed. Reid and Bentley, 1996) suggest the following are 'the main types of non-fiction genre': recount, report, procedure, explanation, exposition and discussion. 'Children who recognise which genre they are reading, and when the author has changed to a different genre (for example from report to exposition), are more likely to read with understanding and to bring a critical eye to the writing.' Readers of non-fiction need to be able to ask themselves a set of questions when encountering that text. Firstly, they need to establish that they are indeed reading non-fiction, then they should have sufficient analytical skills to ask if the text is written in one of the genres or types listed above. They will, of course, need teaching about the features which characterise each type, and will benefit from regular practice in recognising those features. They should also be writing in those text types, for specific purposes, re-emphasising once more the relationship between reading and writing.

Through these straightforward exercises, pupils should begin to think more carefully about the differences in types of text, and to understand that every text requires a slightly different approach in the ways meaning can be made from them. Research into reading, most significantly that of Lunzer and Gardner in *The Effective Use of Reading* (1979), has shown that fiction and non-fiction require very different approaches, and children actually have to be shown specifically how to make meaning from the multiplicity of non-fiction texts they will encounter in and beyond school.

The chart listing differences between fiction and non-fiction texts (Figure 5.3) could be shared with more able readers to assist them in making reflections on their own reading practice. Ironically, good readers of fiction might not always be the best readers of non-fiction, because good readers have developed their skill of involving themselves in books, expecting to make continuous sense over great swathes of text.

Pupils have to be aware of *why* they are engaging with the non-fiction text, and what it is they are expecting to take from it. They need to learn that non-fiction demands an **interrupted read**, with moments of reflection to check on the continued relevance of what is being studied, in contrast to the cumulative, continuous read they would undertake with a fiction text. They might need to employ **skimming and scanning** techniques, looking for particular clues in the text, rather than reading every word. Many texts use **typographical devices** to separate and emphasise the different aspects of knowledge being conveyed: bold type; headings; sub headings; italics – the use of these often differ from text to text.

Knowledge will be required for the most effective use of the contents page, the index, glossaries and references to other texts. They may need to **make notes** to remember the details of what is being studied, because there is no logical development of the material, as in most fiction.

Good readers, like all other readers, need to be made aware of the formal language employed in many non-fiction, information texts, which differ considerably from the manner in which their fiction texts are constructed.

> Fiction is more personal than non-fiction; its language is more accessible and closer to the conventions of everyday speech (dialogue rarely figures in non-fiction texts). Also fiction makes much greater use of pronouns and much less use of the impersonal and passive constructions that characterise non-fiction texts. (Perera, 1992)

They probably need to hear passages read aloud, to establish how the unusual word order can be deconstructed. It is not unusual to find the subject at the end of the sentence:

e.g. 'The remains and shape of animals and plants buried for millions of years in the earth's rocks are called fossils.'

or extended phrases between subject and verb:

e.g. 'The agouti, a very nervous 20 inch, 6 pound rodent that lives in South America, can leap twenty feet from a sitting position.'

Non-fiction, information books regularly use passive constructions:

e.g. 'Holidays were taken at seaside resorts.'

and others employ a 'timeless' present tense:

e.g. 'Ants use their antennae to find food.'

There are now increasing numbers of non-fiction big books being published, which should help teachers address these reading tactics more directly. The National Literacy Strategy will encourage their widespread use during the next few years, and the related INSET programme will enable teachers to become more confident in teaching specific linguistic differences. All pupils should, as a consequence, have more opportunity to study the ways in which texts are constructed. More able readers, once they have been apprised of the points of language they are seeking, should be encouraged to find further examples for themselves.

Other features of textual study

Often overlooked or not recognised for its proper importance is the teaching of how illustrations and diagrams work in non-fiction texts. The necessity of giving real attention to this area of textual understanding was impressed on me by a more able Key Stage 2 boy, who showed me a political cartoon by Steve Bell in *The Guardian*, and asked me what it meant. It was clear that he needed to have some sense of the political context in which the cartoon appeared, but he also required an explanation of the symbolic force of the various pictorial features of the text. This picture was drawn during the Major government 1992–95, and featured John Major wearing baggy, unsightly 'Y front' underpants. We had to make a clear association with the comic character Superman, then explore the ironic comment the cartoonist was making. Layers of meaning in the picture then became more readily accessible, and the boy enjoyed in a more accomplished manner later, similar representations of John Major!

Many text books published to support learning in school subjects employ diagrams and pictures which are not, on first contact, always meaningful to readers. Pupils have been known to ignore the illustrations altogether, or have not realised that an association has to be made with the written text. Some diagrams are intended to be helpful, but their placing on the page does not make them clearly relevant, or they might be drawn in such a way that their own meaning has to be made clearer. When teachers are pointing to specific details on the page in their teaching of these texts, they should also make clear reference to the purpose of the pictures, why they have been included and what extra they are supposed to be contributing to the meaning-making. More able readers should be making these associations a feature of their approach to non-fiction texts and be ready, as a matter of course, to ask what they can gain from the illustrative material.

Just as it is necessary for Key Stage 1 pupils to be given increasing access to the fuller meaning of a range of texts, such as comics, newspapers, magazines, advertisements, computer games, so their Key Stage 2 counterparts should be growing in their insights of those materials. More able readers should be familiar with the sections of newspapers. They should be able to explain how their favourite comics or magazines are divided, and begin to explain how those sections are constructed, either in terms of pictures and written text, or in the way language is employed. I have looked in more detail at these skills in the final chapter.

Conclusion

I have been told by primary teachers that the approach to reading outlined and recommended above is commendable and could contribute to a programme they would like to teach. Yet they are concerned about disadvantaging their pupils who have to be tested at the end of the Key Stage. I would like to suggest that, far from distracting pupils from the tests, they will ultimately be much better prepared. The test is only, after all, another text type and pupils should be able to cope with any form of reading suitable for their age group. The most able readers should bring their skills to bear on the test situation as they would to any other reading context.

They might find the test rather more tedious than most of the work they are given, but they will certainly not be disadvantaged.

In 1996 Level 6, that which will properly reflect a more able reader, will be assessed separately in recognition of the fact that it has proved almost impossible to write questions that will challenge the experienced reader sufficiently and, at the same time, not daunt the newly independent reader. Thus children entered for the higher level will need to focus on detail of plot, character and action in order to make judgements, predictions and draw conclusions. They will also be confident at distinguishing fact from opinion and appropriate use of language, vocabulary choices, metaphor and simile. They will be prolific readers of a wide range of material. (Reid and Bentley, 1996)

Key Stages 3 and 4

I have continually stressed throughout this book that more able pupils arriving at secondary school should be quickly identified and allocated tasks which reflect the highest expectations of them. As part of the early familiarisation process of pupils with the school and teachers with the pupils, English departments should ask their pupils to write responses to a sheet like the Mind Map of the Reader in Figure 5.4. At the end of every term or half yearly, as they pass through the school, pupils should repeat the exercise. From the responses teachers can trace if pupils are displaying evidence of real reading growth, following up their findings with personal advice and counselling, as necessary.

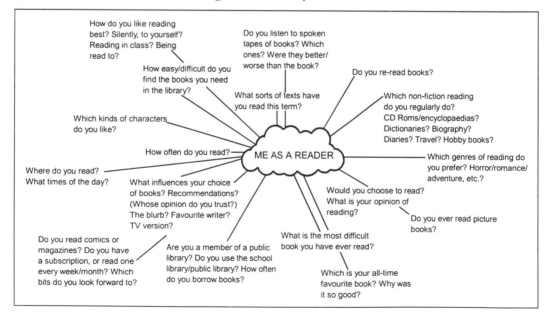

Figure 5.4 Mind Map of the Reader (thanks to Jeanette Mackie Lord Williams's School, Thame)

Secondary English departments have to be very clear about what they mean by the term 'readers' and then put in place the teaching and support which will help pupils to attain that goal. Too often in Key Stage 3 books are placed in front of classes of pupils because they happen to be in the stock cupboard! Year on year, there has been little evidence that many departments are asking questions about the suitability of the texts they are employing, or whether all members of the department are clear about which reading purposes the texts are serving and encouraging.

The least differentiated activity which many English departments employ is to share a text with a whole class. More years ago than I care to admit, I remember sitting in a grammar school classroom, an enthusiastic and avid reader, having to endure a text which I believe was called *The Shetland Bus*. I would not have chosen this text for myself, but I never knew why it was chosen for me. We had to read around the class, and even though it was a grammar school there were boys who read more slowly than I was capable of doing by myself. So I read ahead, because a book in which it was already proving a struggle to maintain an interest would have been even more tedious at their pace. We were asked closed 'comprehension' questions around the class, to ensure a superficial understanding, and wrote one or two pieces about the characters. I was not, in any respect, consciously a better or more skilled reader as a consequence of this engagement. I had added another title to the list of texts I had read, but otherwise recognised no benefit from the contact. Much shared reading in secondary English departments is still of that nature.

It is not my intention to ban the shared class text, even if that injunction was in my power. It is my objective to ensure that, where class texts are placed in front of all the pupils in any classroom, there are planned activities which enable pupils to move at an appropriate pace through the text, to know the purposes for which the text has been chosen, and to engage in activities with others which bring the possible meanings of the text into full focus. This objective does not rule out whole class work, or even whole class reading of portions of the text (the beginning of the text is an obvious example). More able readers in mixed ability classes, particularly, but also in ability sets, must be sufficiently challenged by the text, must have access to a range of approaches to make alternative readings, and should take from their work insights and skills which they are capable of articulating in the reflection they will make of their work.

Young people in Key Stage 3 are at a difficult transitional point in their lives and experience. Teenage readers can prove challenging for teachers attempting to meet their needs and interests at the same time. Their moods and concerns are capable of rapid change and their progress cannot be discerned in straight lines. It is not unusual for them to read utterly trivial and undemanding material alongside texts which could well be considered 'adult'. More able readers are not protected from these adolescent swings by any magical powers; they are just as likely to display the same symptoms. Teachers and parents hoping to continue supporting and challenging these youngsters have to show patience and be sensitive about the best moments to recommend new reading. If the culture of discussing reading and reflecting seriously on personal habits and practice is well established, the progression of individuals might be easier to sustain. If pupils have not been used to these ways of working, the school ought to be establishing new habits and ways of review.

A further problem is that posed by the reading behaviour of boys. Even good readers reduce their reading of fiction, and growing interests in other subjects or out of school activities distract them further. There is little to be gained by bullying or cajoling them back into required reading practice! It is enough that teachers continue to seek areas of mutual engagement, when they are able to find occasional texts which can hold the reader, and to ensure that the work and learning which is planned for the reading encounter continues the reader's progress. Keeping a watching brief on reluctant but able readers is a clear enough message to them that they are still important, and that their development is still a matter of concern to the staff.

Both of the problem areas outlined above are good reasons why the more able should not have their supervised school reading defined entirely by the class text. They should either have their reading diet supplemented by group work on a regular basis, or have a clear individual support programme, through which they are able to benefit from structured discussion about their reading in the same way as members of groups. An effective starting point in this programme is to encourage pupils to have their current reading texts available in the classroom. I am always impressed with the range of texts evident in classrooms where the pupils are expected to bring them along; but, more importantly, they allow any teacher a convenient way of superficial monitoring, and the opportunity for a short conversation about the choices being made. They also allow quick, unobtrusive, 'end of the lesson' chances for pupils to talk aloud about their texts, recommending them – or otherwise – using increasingly sophisticated reasons.

English departments which have **reading lists** prepared for their pupils are already beginning to make a statement about the areas of reading they think their pupils should encounter. A reading list should be a carefully constructed support instrument and draw on the widest knowledge of texts the department can gather. This might mean using the services of the school librarian, or the county schools' library service, because their personnel are invariably well-informed about current engaging texts for the different age and ability groups. The list really ought to be more than just the names of texts and authors, to stimulate further textual consideration. Attempting to place the titles within *genre* groupings should be a challenge for the department and the pupils, because they are not easily decided or exclusive categories. Reviewing existing book lists could be a task given to more able readers, both to rework the available material, possibly placing books in more than one section, and to add titles not included. There are probably a number of schools with excellent book lists, which ought to be shared in English network groups. In the Appendix I have included a good example known to me from Lord Williams's School at Thame.

Sue Maguire, a teacher at Banbury School, supervised a project, with my help, to draw up a new approach to book lists for more able readers called *Reading Well*. Our intention was to avoid recommending only 'classical' texts for more assured readers from Year 7 onwards, and to bridge the gap between adolescent fiction and more adult material. We also wanted the reading of one text to set off interests or ideas, which could be supplemented by further reading of related texts. The same title could be associated with a whole range of related texts. There is a detailed set of genre-related titles which concludes the booklet. Finally, we wanted the booklet to be given to more able readers, who could then use its suggestions in their own way, and possibly contribute to further updates. An example from this booklet is given in the Appendix.

Range of reading

Many good readers at the beginning of Key Stage 3 might already have formed some firm views about the sorts of texts they enjoy. They could have read their way through as many novels by Jan Mark, or Anne Fine, or Terry Pratchett, or J.R.R. Tolkien, or Robert Westall as they can find. A few might even have reached the stage of being devoted to the works of Thomas Hardy or Jane Austen, or the Sherlock Holmes stories. Once again, as I have stressed at all stages, pupils should be given every chance to talk about what they know of their reading. Why do they so naturally enjoy the work of their chosen writers? What is it that they seek in further texts by those authors? Are the experiences contained within those works escapist, or do they relate to concerns shared by the reader, or do they touch on other associations? How did they discover the texts in the first place? What would they want to convey about them to other readers?

Some recommended textual study for Key Stage 3

Teachers often wish to urge their pupils into further reading, but do not feel they know enough about which texts would be suitable or sufficiently engaging, beyond a traditional canon. A few English departments have established shared reading programmes for staff, where they all agree to read one or two texts recently published for young people each term, and then hold a session for making their recommendations to colleagues. There are almost endless numbers of activities which could be thought up to undertake with worthwhile texts. Most of the following titles, published in the last few years, have proved to be a 'good read' for more able readers, and lend themselves as extension study alongside other texts. Some have been popular with boys, of all abilities. They are not all intrinsically difficult books, although a few are textually demanding and might need teacher support, but they do all lend themselves to helpful and supportive comparative readings. Teachers should consider ways in which they might set up programmes of independent study using these, or similar, resources.

Roger J. Green's *The Throttlepenny Murder* is a dark, gripping and lively thriller, set in the nineteenth century. It reflects the thinking of its 13-year-old heroine, who is mistakenly accused of murder. This could be read alongside any of Philip Pullman's 'Sally Lockhart' series, particularly *The Ruby in the Smoke*, also set in the nineteenth century, but with a very different female central character.

Nightjohn by Gary Paulsen is a short, tight, intense novel about slavery in the southern states of the USA. It is also about the liberating powers of education. It could be used as a perfect companion text to Barbara Smucker's *Underground to Canada*, which is studied in many Key Stage 3 classes. All Gary Paulsen's novels, *Hatchet*, *Tasting the Thunder* and *Mr Tucket*, are strongly written, with much action but well-drawn characterisation, which appeals to both female and male readers. Paulsen draws heavily on American literature for his background and themes, which suggests another possible area of comparative work with texts written about themes more familiar in Great Britain.

Peter Dickinson is another assured and popular story-teller. His well-known *AK* deals with the difficult subject of boy soldiers in an African war. This should be read with *Gulf* by Robert Westall, which also explores the place of a young boy in war, but from a most unusual perspective.

The Diary of Anne Frank has been, rightly, extremely popular since its original publication and English departments still find it to be an intelligent and poignant model of autobiography, locked into a harrowing situation. Most girls feel a genuine association with it. Other texts of comparable quality which have more in common than just being about young women are: *Zlata's Diary* by Zlata Filipovic, dealing with life in contemporary war-torn Sarajevo; Elizabeth Laird's *Kiss the Dust*, exploring similar 'ethnic cleansing' issues from the point of view of the Kurds; *The Frozen Waterfall* by Gaye Hicyilmaz looks at the situation of the 'outsider', a young Turkish girl in Switzerland; *No Turning Back* by Beverley Naidoo observes the lives of young people on the streets of post-apartheid Johannesburg; and – possibly most problematic of all – M. E. Kerr's *Deliver Us from Evie* involves two girls in a small community in Mississippi who fall in love, and encounter appalling homophobia as a consequence. Readers who enjoy this text might also enjoy Jeanette Winterson's *Oranges are not the Only Fruit*.

A few novels dealing with contemporary social issues in an adult manner, but written specifically for young people, are: Berlie Doherty's *The Snakestone*, throwing light on adoption and identity; *Dear Nobody*, by the same author, a painful and very honest consideration of teenage pregnancy, which has genuinely moved young lads who have been encouraged to read it; *Wolf*, by Gillian Cross, has a multi-layered plot involving the IRA, and should be read alongside Bernard MacLaverty's study of Northern Irish life, *Cal*; Lesley Howarth's *Weather Eye*, focuses on environmental issues, while her book *The Flower King*, combines a mystery with fantasy, yet still manages to explore real concerns to do with the old, and the nature of fame! June Oldham, in her very sensitive and sad novel *Escape*, studies the pain and betrayal of incest.

Two very uncompromising stories, which deal, respectively, with hopelessness and drugs are Robert Swindell's *Stone Cold* and Melvin Burgess's *Junk*. *The Baby and Fly Pie*, by Melvyn Burgess, is about gangs of homeless and dispossessed youngsters who roam the outskirts of a city; it has a clear theme of hope running through it, but is a difficult book for some young people to read.

Novels which share themes of life in war time, and also have an element of comparison across time, either through flashback or setting lives against each other, are Michelle Magorian's *A Little Love Song*, Mary Rayner's *The Echoing Green* and Linda Newbury's trilogy *The Shouting Wind*.

Finally, there is a selection of books, worthy of study by young people who have developed real fluency and confidence with texts, which do not readily fall into easy categorisation. The first recommendation is a series by Sylvia Waugh about some strange characters called *The Mennyms*. A real challenge to pupils is to ask them to suggest a genre for these books! Two texts which reward careful language study are *Ultramarine* by Jenny Nimmo and *The Mysterious Mr Ross* by Vivien Alcock. Both are strange, almost fantasy tales, which slide gently in and out of reality and will bear deconstruction. *Eva,* by Peter Dickinson, is a grossly underrated work which, quite literally, has the power to get under a reader's skin! Every page keeps you alive and prickling. It has far more impact than any Point Horror book could achieve, yet with much more humanity.

Jostein Gaarder has become a best-selling author with his books for teenagers tackling ideas of philosophy. He is the sort of writer readers either enjoy enormously, or they find him impossible to deal with. His most notable work is *Sophie's World*, but the *The Solitaire Mystery* has a clear philosophical theme too, which could appeal to the same audience.

The very last reference is to a series of novels which are likely to become regarded as very important works in the coming years. Philip Pullman's *Northern Lights* has already won a number of literary prizes. It is the first book in the trilogy *His Dark Materials* which explores massive themes of good and evil in a mature and difficult manner, but in a most readable style. Pullman remains, above all else, a marvellous story-teller. Good readers are likely to get excited about this text and their teachers will want to explore its ideas and delineations in detail.

Of course, these divisions and groupings of texts have been arbitrarily determined by myself, because I discovered these particular similarities between them. The resonances texts create are different for different readers, and able readers given this sort of task should be encouraged to make their own decisions about which texts might be placed together for whatever critical reasons.

Organisation for reading

How pupils are organised in classes or groups, to maximise learning and critical development in relation to texts, can depend on a number of factors. If the department groups by ability, some identification of the more able has already taken place, although the fact that they might be together in a 'top set' is not of itself the complete answer for supplying their most effective support. In those departments where pupils are assigned to mixed ability groups, there has to be provision for the more able to be brought together within at least an occasional group arrangement in the class, or some other separate system operating beyond timetabled English lessons. Another factor likely to affect the department's management of this able group will depend on how many have been identified for these special needs. If there are clearly four or five such pupils in each year, joined by a few who could be regarded as benefiting from being at the 'fringe', then it might actually be possible to bring them together for some lessons. They could certainly meet for lunchtime or after school activities, and even form 'sub groups' of their own, for reading and swapping shared texts. Where only one or two pupils are evident in a year group, or where one or two are identified in some but not all years in the school, bringing them together will prove more difficult, as will planning worthwhile, shared interest activities for pupils of disparate ages.

I was once talking to a teacher at the end of a lesson, when a shy, able Year 9 girl approached us to ask if she could talk to somebody about *Jane Eyre*, which she had just finished reading, of her own volition. Based on that moment, the department believed it ought to make proper arrangements for that girl and similar pupils.

Poetry

Poetry study at Key Stage 3 is a variable lottery. I know of some English departments which plan no teaching of poetry whatsoever in Years 7 to 9, except for the dramatic poetry of the compulsory Shakespeare play (and even then the actual poetry is rarely foremost). Some departments use poetry as a device on which to base their pre-twentieth-century understanding. A few teachers have given a great deal of time to thinking about the implications of poetry teaching, and setting up ways of engaging the interest of young people in the early years of secondary education. The problem is made worse because virtually all pupils have had such an inadequate preparation in thinking about and being made familiar with poetry that too many negative responses have grown to begin successful study of poetry at that time.

Teaching poetry also worries some English teachers. They are concerned that the supposedly 'difficult' material will be beyond the scope of their pupils and fail to gain their approval. In those circumstances, they either choose material which is too undemanding, or they adopt a dogged, 'we must get through this' attitude which results in joyless, dutiful lessons. More risks really do have to be taken and teachers should be prepared to allow their classes to take more control of the meaning-making. I have sat in a lesson of very able Year 9 pupils wading their way, line by line, through a Wilfred Owen poem and wondered why they were ever given that material. At the other extreme, I have seen a mixed ethnic Year 8 class, mainly of boys, including speakers of English as an alternative language, excited by an imaginative study of 'The Charge of the Light Brigade', which developed into a fierce debate about imperialism and patriotism.

Some of the best study I have seen in this difficult area has involved sharing all the perceptions of poetry that pupils have brought to the classroom. They were invited to 'brainstorm' all their thoughts on the topic and explore what experiences might have led to those reactions. They were challenged to remember as much as they could about the poetry that had been learned, consciously or otherwise, from their past, whilst being made aware of the many sources of poetry around them, accessible in their day to day lives. The more able learners in this setting were invited to look at a selection of poetry texts – collections by particular poets and anthologies – the department owned in its stock cupboard. They considered the dates of publication, the titles of the collections, the covers and their presentation, the contents and range of the featured poets. Most interestingly, they studied in detail the Preface pages of the different collections, to consider and work out how they – as poetry readers – had been positioned in relation to the texts, and to learn what those compilers want their readers to believe poetry might be.

Some examples are fascinatingly different. *Vigorous Verse* (a wonderfully evocative title), compiled by W. R. S. McIntyre in 1963, begins:

> This book presents a collection of verse which it is hoped will arouse the interest of boys and girls who think poetry is dull, and will give further pleasure to those who already find poetry attractive. All may gain some realisation that poetry can embrace a wide range of experience, from the simple and humorous to the more significant and serious.

David Orme, in his introduction to *The Windmill Book of Poetry* (1987), states a different, and oddly mixed, perspective:

> This anthology is arranged so poems with similar themes, or written in the same forms, can complement and comment on each other, but broad categorising has been avoided.

Later he makes a desperate plea, clearly based on unhappy experiences: 'At all costs poems should not be set as comprehension exercises.'

A fundamentally different approach is shown by Wendy Cope in her much more personal introduction to *Is That the New Moon? Poems by Women Poets*, published in 1989:

> Most people can't be bothered with poetry, least of all with contemporary poetry. At social gatherings, I am tempted to avoid mentioning that I have anything to do with it ... Somehow they have become convinced that poetry is too difficult, too mysterious, not for them. They haven't had the good fortune to find out that reading poetry can help you live your life.

Yet that important challenge is left dangling, without further explanation.

This extremely tiny selection of openings could bring about potentially illuminating discussion for a group of able readers, helping them to reflect on their approach to poetry, and encouraging a careful reading of the examples they will study. This preparation is not intended to prevent the close reading and making of meaning of poetry itself; quite the contrary. To find their own distinctive way of working effectively with poetry, however, they will need to open their minds to a range of responses, as well as learning sets of questions to put to new poems they encounter. The second set of critical tools is too regularly taught without much acknowledgement of the former.

Much of the poetry teaching which takes place in Key Stage 3 involves single poems, either being studied individually to explore the use of, for instance, simile, onomatopoeia or rhythm, or to compare with another single poem with a similar theme. More able readers should be encouraged to seek particular poets who have something special to convey to them. Teachers can recommend collections that pupils can test for themselves or provide lists of poets who have written about themes and topics popular with the reader. Once again, it will be difficult to match writer and reader successfully unless the teacher knows the pupil well, and the department has the means to follow through recommendations by monitoring the reading and extent of meaning-making.

Non-fiction study

Throughout their school lives, pupils should be made increasingly aware of the relationship between reading and writing. In the secondary school the more able readers should be increasingly encouraged to draw on different textual sources for their models of writing, possibly collecting banks of material from a number of different sources. The prize-winning NATE resource *Klondyke Kate and other Non-fiction Texts*, produced by Barbara Bleiman, Sabrina Broadbent and Michael Simons in 1995, is an excellent text, which teachers could not only use in their classrooms with more able readers, but could use as the starting point for a similar collection of their own. The pupils themselves should be encouraged to contribute, and to devise the questions and approaches to be applied to their articles or extracts. The department will have been really successful when it is able to make a broad range of non-fiction materials as enjoyable and accessible for its more accomplished readers as it is likely to achieve with its more mainstream literary examples. Being a good reader should not mean being restricted to a limited amount of fiction.

Chapter 6

How to Challenge and Improve the Writing of More Able Writers

There is general agreement that the teaching of writing in primary schools has not been as well developed as it ought to have been. OFSTED inspection findings for the past few years have continually highlighted the teaching of writing as a serious weakness. In 1976, Nancy Martin and colleagues, in a Schools Council report, were claiming:

> The trouble with most school writing is that it is not genuine communication. When adults write they are usually trying to tell someone something he doesn't already know; when children write in school they are usually writing for someone who, they are well aware, knows better than they do what they are trying to say and who is concerned to evaluate their attempt to say it. Even when they are writing a story, when the teacher does not know better than they do what they are saying, the response of the teacher is so often to the surface features of spelling, punctuation and handwriting. So, once again the teacher is seen as assessor and not as someone being communicated with. (Martin *et al.*, 1976)

In 1995 Lewis and Wray of the Exel Project, in *Developing Children's Non-fiction Writing* (Scholastic, 1995), quote a contemporary OFSTED summary report for the teaching of English which claims 'much remains to be done to improve the writing competence of pupils of all ages'. It goes on to say that 'writing standards were depressed by excessive copying and a lack of demand for sustained, independent and extended writing'.

Most writing in the infant and primary school is a form of 'downloading' of all the available ideas and responses contained in the child's mind, without any form of discernment or rigorous filtering before that material reaches the paper. Too many children do not know the difference between speaking and writing, and set about compiling written texts in the same ways they might derive spoken texts. Indeed, much of what many pupils write down could be one part of a conversation. Pupils of all abilities have to be helped in their decision making, to choose which areas of their knowledge and insights are necessary to fulfil the purposes of the writing, the style in which it should be composed, and how well they convey what they are intending to the selected audience – all intellectual processes which the writer should be controlling.

Writing tasks in the primary school are virtually always decided by the teacher, without much consideration of the range of texts available. I have a sense that there is far too much writing in primary schools, mostly set by teachers to prove that an engagement has taken place between the teacher and the pupil, for the benefit of the parents. Too little writing teaching has taken place to improve the actual writing competence and the learning children can do through writing.

Across all four Key Stages the main challenge for teachers is to establish pupil control of the writing process, supporting them as they move towards the status of increasingly independent writers who are capable of making intellectual decisions in the form of real choices about their written communication. The writer should grow in awareness of the **purpose** of the writing, the intended **audience** for any writing – real or imaginary – and the **style** of writing which suits those two criteria best. If children in Key Stage 1 are expected to be working in this manner, it follows that the proportional sense of mastery pupils in Key Stage 4 should be displaying is enormous.

Writing in the infant school

Some able children arrive at school already writing, others will quickly understand, in that new supportive and stimulating setting, that making marks on paper has a vital permanence and can be the means of conveying all sorts of information. Those able children are already likely to know of a variety of texts which contain different messages. I have an example of a newspaper written by a child not yet old enough for school, which is an example of this knowledge. A child's developing understanding of the way various messages are composed, the reasons why writers might want to compose them, and the effects they are intended to have on their readers should be the business of the school from that time.

Children who have recognised that writing is functional require models of the many types of texts available to them, to begin studying the features which characterise those types so that they can begin writing in the same manner. This requirement raises three problems:

- Most pupils encounter far more fiction than non-fiction in the earliest stages of schooling, which means that teachers should be seeking to ensure children are able to experience the widest and best balanced reading schedule.
- If pupils are to study texts to learn from them, the texts have to be worth learning from. Particularly from the first stages, pupils have to be in contact with texts which are good representatives of their type.
- Teachers have to be aware of the importance they have in 'modelling' the texts

they have selected, why they are selecting the parts they do, and what learning they wish to bring about in their pupils. Once again, 'differentiation by outcome' is not an approach to learning which can be left to chance.

This development in language teaching is what used to be vaguely known as 'knowledge about language', which the LINC project (see p.34) attempted to explore and define more carefully.

When thinking about children's school experience of language it is helpful to bear in mind the three ways in which language forms part of their learning. During the course of their education children are learning:

- *through* language;
- *to use* language;
- and *about* language.

The LINC project was able to demonstrate that children are capable of learning about language – not through dry, decontextualised exercises, but through real study and growing insight of worthwhile texts – from a much earlier age than many teachers had previously thought possible. A set of case studies illustrating how well young learners produced supposedly 'difficult' non-chronological texts, in *Looking into Language*, are introduced in the following way:

> The teachers have introduced models of the genre for the children to engage with. With these models, teachers are able to tease out what the children already know about how writing is differentiated by audience and purpose, and how such dynamics influence the choices we make within different 'levels' of the language system – layout, discourse structure, cohesion, grammar, vocabulary and so on. As far as the writing tasks themselves have been concerned, these have been located firmly within the children's own orbit of interests and concerns – a well known fairy story, a favourite meal, an endangered environment, their own school. (Bain *et al.*, 1992)

So, as well as purpose, audience and style being necessary elements in the pupil's knowledge about his or her writing, there should also be a clear sense of **context**.

The planned National Literacy Strategy, to be introduced to schools from 1998, should help to make learning about many sorts of texts more specific for the youngest pupils and raise expectations about the standards of writing they are capable of producing. Yet even in this potential improved setting, more able writers should still be properly identified and encouraged to make all possible progress.

Jenny Monk, a former advisory teacher, now Senior Lecturer at Westminster College, Oxford, undertook research with two classes of Year 1 and 2 children, to explore their capability of writing argument texts. A section entitled 'The Language of Argument in the Writing of Young Children' in *Looking into Language* (Bain *et al.*, 1992), records the experience of these pupils, who were supported and 'scaffolded' through their writing about issues concerned with an environmental problem. The pupils structured successful arguments, including points of view in which they did not necessarily believe. Figure 6.1 shows the stages an individual able writer went through in producing a piece of argument writing, after discussing the contrasting issues with an adult. The child chose to write separate paragraphs representing each view, although she was aware that there was an alternative way of structuring the piece using sentences which began 'on the one hand', and later contained phrases beginning 'alternatively', or 'on the other hand'. The growth of this pupil's thinking skills, as well as her writing development, can clearly be seen in this process.

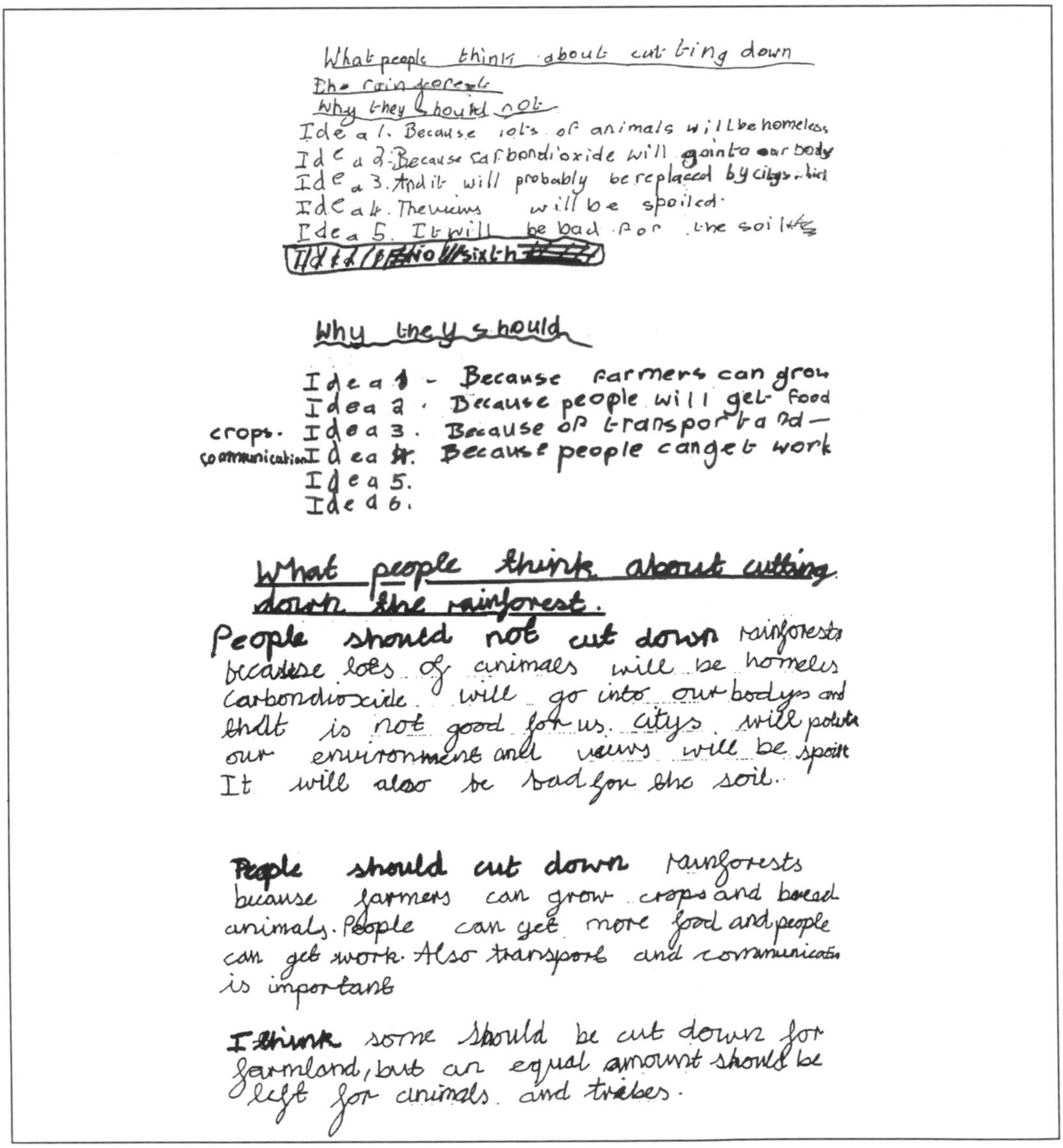

What people think about cutting down the rainforest

Why they should not

Idea 1. Because lots of animals will be homeless

Idea 2. Because carbondioxide will go into our body

Idea 3. And it will probably be replaced by citys which

Idea 4. The views will be spoiled.

Idea 5. It will be bad for the soil

Why they should

Idea 1 - Because farmers can grow crops.

Idea 2. Because people will get food

Idea 3. Because of transport and communication

Idea 4. Because people can get work

Idea 5.

Idea 6.

What people think about cutting down the rainforest.

People should not cut down rainforests because lots of animals will be homeless carbondioxide will go into our bodys and that is not good for us. citys will polute our environment and views will be spoilt It will also be bad for the soil.

People should cut down rainforests because farmers can grow crops and bread animals. People can get more food and people can get work. Also transport and communication is important

I think some should be cut down for farmland, but an equal amount should be left for animals and tribes.

Figure 6.1

This evidence is very strong. We have to accept that children really can deal with the whole range of available text types from the very earliest stages of their writing, given the right support and being shown the clearest models. Overwhelmingly in infant schools they are asked to produce only fiction, news and recount writing. If all children can tackle supposedly 'difficult' texts, we should be expecting more able writers to be writing all sorts of texts in a knowledgeable way.

Types of text

I deliberately began by exploring a non-fiction form of writing, because narrative is the most usual form of writing – just as fiction is the most common beginning of reading – taught in primary school. Children exposed to a number of stories quickly realise that there are characteristic features of beginnings, that some form of action is expected to take place in the body of the story, and the characters involved regularly 'live happily ever after.' Either through overt teaching or sub-consciously through absorption resulting from familiarity, these children have learned the simplest details of narrative structure, to form the foundations of their subsequent development. Non-fiction simply does not benefit from the same amount of re-telling or from any specific focus being placed on it through deliberate teaching.

In the past many teachers have attempted to explore other forms of text beyond narrative. They have taught letters, for instance, or diaries. The problem has been that letters can be written in all sorts of different ways. There are formal and informal letters, yet informal letters can be further sub-divided into the chatty between friends, or grateful to granny, or in the form of a list to a business acquaintance. All are slightly different. Formal letters might be requesting, complaining or explaining; again necessitating different approaches in tone and register. Teachers need more secure knowledge about *text types*, rather than forms of text, on which to build a sound writing programme.

Recent research into genre theory has suggested that there are six types of text – **recount, report, procedure, explanation, persuasion or exposition** and **discussion** – which have been identified as the most used and important types of writing in our culture. They are not the only types of text, and while they have individually identifiable features, they are not exclusive, there are areas of overlap. It is, however, possible to teach many features of these types and articulate with pupils the aspects which they can address when improving their writing in them. Quite clearly, the dialogue with more able writers can begin at an earlier stage and be conducted at a level which continues to challenge them appropriately.

The writing process

Most adults are not capable of writing more than the most trivial pieces of writing (e.g. lists, reminders, simple memos) without reworking the material in some way to express precisely what is being meant. Children, too, need to realise that most writing is not 'straight off' and their first attempts are unlikely to yield the results they want to convey. The initial writing down of our ideas should be regarded as the first gathering of material, more or less in the planned eventual sequence, but with the clear proviso that those words are capable of change. Only tests and examinations call on pupils to offer their best shot on the first attempt!

This process, known as **drafting**, has to be established early, and has to be seen by the pupils as much more than making a 'fair copy' of their original untidy version. Sometimes the first attempt will need only minor adjusting to achieve the required outcome, but there could well be occasions on which the whole first attempt needs to be abandoned and the topic approached in a wholly new way. Pupils have to be helped to see that this way of writing is the proper response to writing tasks, and it is an essential feature of the intellectual filtering that writers, of whatever age, should be employing.

Drafting is better undertaken in social settings, where writers have a chance to discuss their intentions, try out their approaches and listen to the advice and criticism of others on the same enterprise. Once again, this way of working should not be utterly exclusive and rule out the occasions when pupils will have to make their own way unaided, but it ought to be applied whenever possible and become the accepted manner in all classrooms. Pupils might work together in pairs, or 'writing clubs', small groups identified for particular learning and supportive purposes, and sometimes – particularly when the pupils are younger – as a whole class.

If the culture of writing in classrooms can change to recognise that the real work should be taking place at the stage of composition, where the penultimate 'draft' becomes the 'battleground' for pupil and teacher interaction, considerable improvement will result. The current practice usually involves pupils constructing writing which is then submitted as a finished piece for marking and assessment. This final version is then written on, in more or less helpful ways, given back to the writer and mostly forgotten or neglected. Much pupils' writing becomes dead matter after if has been dealt with by the teacher, when it should be contributing to further progress. One of the problems preventing this progressive development in infant and junior schools has to do with the resources provided for writing tasks. The pupils are often expected to use one book for their drafting, where that is a requirement, and then asked to write the finished version on a separate piece of paper, or later in the same book, but sometimes at some distance from the original. In this way, pupils have no real record of the writing process they have experienced and the 'drafts' have no real status.

I am suggesting that pupils should be given a broad writing curriculum throughout their school lives, that they should know the names and characteristics of the text types they are practising, and that the separate types should be stored in such a way that it is possible to trace progress in those text types. Perhaps writing of different types can be kept in plastic envelopes, with the drafts firmly attached to the final version, offering clear evidence of the stages children have gone through before they have arrived at what they deem to be a satisfactory conclusion. The assessment record the teacher will be able to call on as a result of this change will be considerable and detailed. There will also be a continual reminder of the necessity of achieving balance in the writing curriculum, if the record of one type becomes more pronounced than the others.

How to support and challenge more able writers

I have been collecting the written work of more able pupils in Key Stage 1 for a few years, but most of it comprises narrative writing and poetry. Either teachers are not considering writing in other types of text as noteworthy, or they are not giving sufficient opportunities for pupils to practise them. A few examples of different sorts of writing from children aged 5 and 6 years old do, however, allow us to consider 'what next' in regard to pupils already capable of working in a more confident manner.

The first example (Figure 6.2) is a letter by a 5-year-old girl, in response to another, older able girl who wrote to her at my request. I believe that able writers should have an opportunity to contact others of similar ability, so that they can share views and interests – often about the books they are encountering, as in this instance – and have real audiences to address. The letter was written unaided. It has an excellent sense of tone and uses an appropriate register. It offers interesting information about the writer and invites the reader to make a personal response at the same level. As the child's teacher I would be delighted with her effort, but I would be encouraging her to think about paragraphing, to draw together similar topics, as her 'what next?' focus.

The next example (Figure 6.3) is a good attempt to write a procedural piece, giving instructions about a set of actions. The Year 2 girl writer has set the piece out in the correct manner and sorted out the steps and stages; she is also an accurate, neat writer – both worthy of celebration. What has not yet been understood, however, is the second person address and the tense of this sort of writing. The final point is correctly written, but the previous six are written in the first person, and the verb 'rinsed' is in the past. I would also want the writer to consider alternatives to the continuous use of 'then' as a connective in this context.

The example in Figure 6.4 is written by a slightly younger writer than the previous example and, in many respects, is already more successful. The language is correct throughout, in the proper person, tense and register. The use of 'and' at the beginning of the final two sections could be eliminated and the teacher will remind the writer of capital letters, but these are less important than the clear understanding of the style – although if the child is to write for a real audience then there can be no escape from the responsibility of accurate prose. The 'what next?' assistance could be in asking the child to write in procedural terms about a another set of instructions.

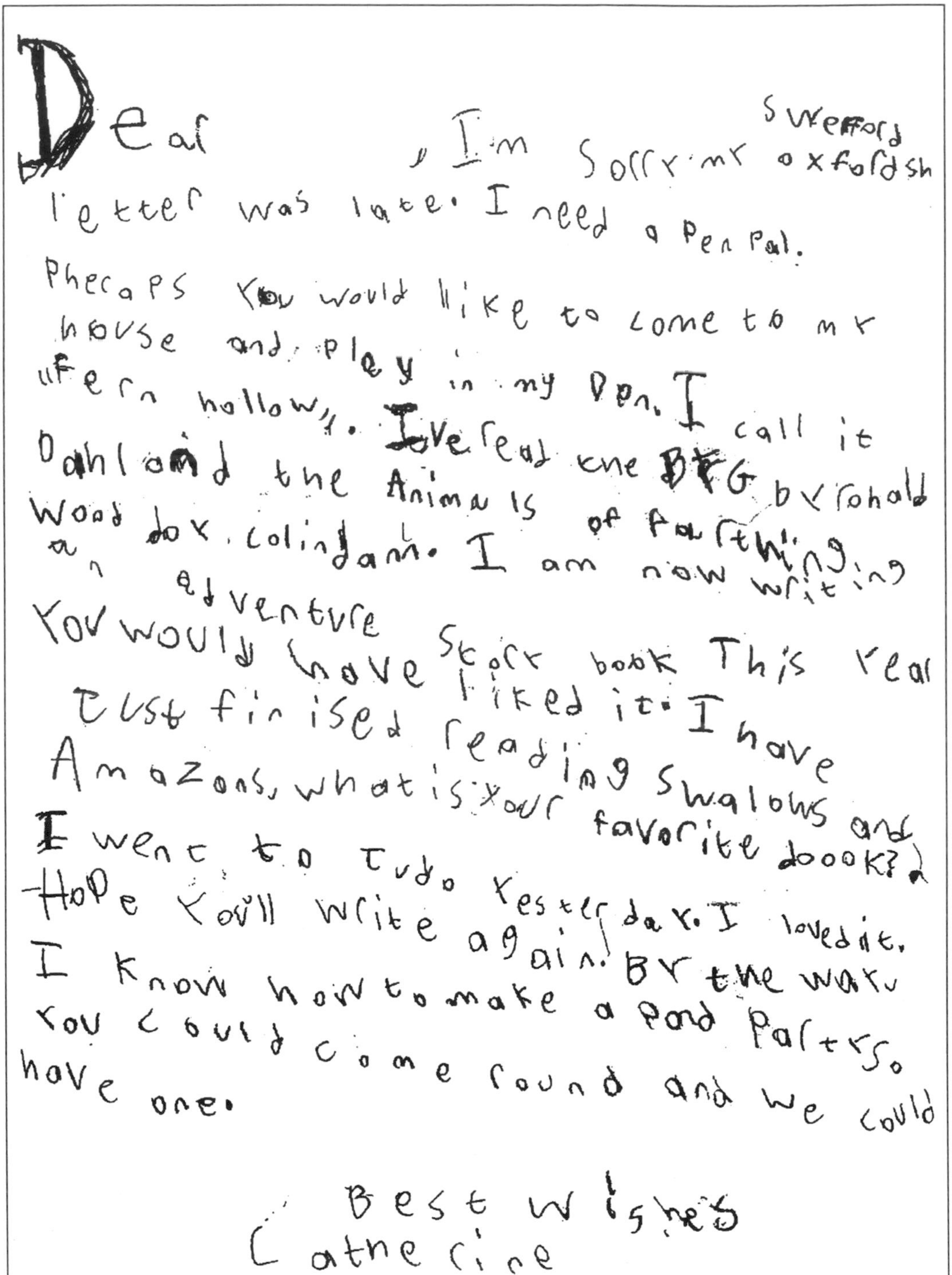

Dear   , I'm sorry my Swefford oxfoldsh letter was late. I need a Pen Pal. Phecaps you would like to come to my house and play in my Den. I call it ufern hollow. I've read the BFG by rohald Dahl and the Animuls of farthing Wood box colindaml. I am now writing an adventure story book This year You would have liked it. I have just finised reading swalows and Amazons, what is your favorite boook? I went to Tudo yesterday. I loved it. Hope youll write again! By the way, I know how to make a pond Parts. you could come round and we could have one.

                 Best wishes
            Catherine

Figure 6.2

Figure 6.3

The fourth example (Figure 6.5) is a piece of script writing by a Year 2 child. Two children were given the opportunity of choosing some sound effects which they thought to be appropriate to their selected theme. They were shown a page of play script and the writer came up with this adventure. She has clearly differentiated the speakers, and integrated sound effect instructions at times. There are a few reactions to events, 'Agggh!' and 'Ahhh', which contribute to a sense of drama, and there is a recognition of a 'narrator' voice over, distinct from the featured characters. The narrative is simple, but has been clearly imagined, suggesting the writer has a sense of radio action. 'What next?' would include pointing out that the characters are delineated, developing the narrator's position and attempting to develop dialogue, which is currently stilted; the characters do not actually talk to each other.

The next example (Figure 6.6) is by a 5-year-old girl. This is a much more recognisable text type in the infant school; a piece of narrative recount. This passage is impressively organised, with a clear chronological structure depending on a clever focus of the angel. There is just a hint of the Biblical source. The 'what next?' tasks would include helping the writer to recognise and compose reported speech, and – not an unusual problem at this stage – finding alternatives for the connective 'then'. There should also be reminders concerning simple features of correct punctuation.

All these examples display a good deal of writer control in response to tasks which are properly understood. They have all been successfully modelled and the writers have been able to distinguish central features of each text type, and then reproduce them in their own way to suit the purposes for which they were intended. If these examples were kept in a writing file, suitably identified by type, it would be interesting for the school to give the children a similar exercise after two years, to discover how much the writers had progressed. The most important success of all these examples is that the children were given a range of writing in which to work. They can only show the full extent of their talents if they are given the full range of opportunities.

Key Stage 2

By this stage pupils should be able to articulate what they are undertaking every time they tackle a piece of writing. They should have a clear idea of the nature of the tasks, who they are addressing and the style and appropriacy of the text type they have chosen. If they are drafting their material, and not all writing contexts will necessitate this approach (end of Key Stage assessment tests are the most obvious examples), they will know that some preliminary discussion should be taking place. They might have considered and studied a possible model of the text type to be adopted, and they will have recognised that their drafts are capable of being significantly changed in the attempt to convey precisely what is meant. More able writers should have these skills at their full disposal, know more about the possible range of texts from which to choose and make realistic commentary on their efforts.

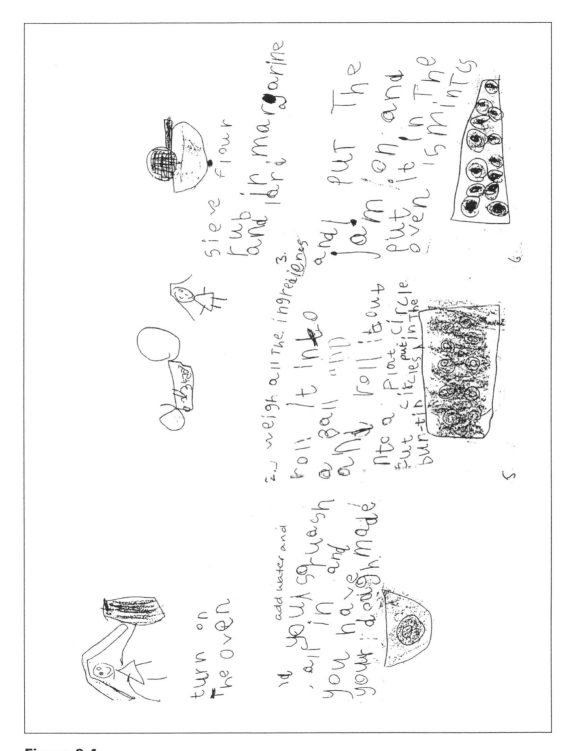

1. sieve flour and lard in margarine

2. weigh all the ingredients

3. roll it into a ball and roll it out into a Plate circle put circles in the bun-tin

4. turn on the oven

id add water and all your squash in and you have your dough made

put the jam on and put it in the oven is minuts

Figure 6.4

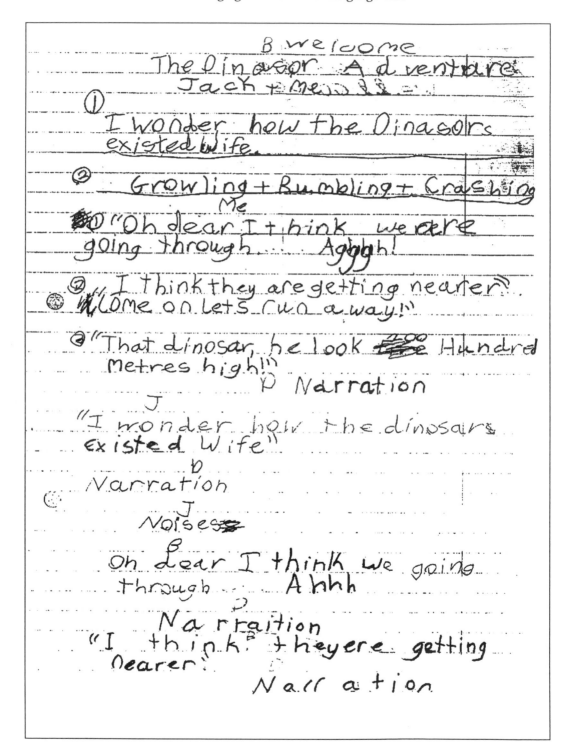

Figure 6.5

one day a Angel came to mary
and she said you will have a baby and
his name will be Jesus but said mary
how can I have a baby if I am not
marred you will marry a man who is
called Joseph Then the angel was gone
the next day mary got marred with
Joseph. the angel went to some shepherds
the angel said to the shepherds a king
is in a cattle shed the shepherds
to the baby. Then the angel went
to some kings and she said to the kings
a king is in the cattle shed the kings
went to the baby. Then the
angel went to the other angels

Figure 6.6

Unfortunately, the reality is more likely to be a continuation of the spoken language masquerading as writing, or – even worse, and a further example was seen in a Year 4 classroom during the week this page was written – worksheets 'about language' which pupils are expected to copy out, filling in missing words. In another classroom, close to Bonfire Night, I saw children attempting to write a piece of journalistic recount of the events of Guy Fawkes' discovery and arrest emerging as narrative fiction, because they were unaware of the distance they were expected to adopt in relation to the scene and could not recognise the voice in which to write. Because children are overwhelmingly used to composing pieces of, so called, 'creative writing' they move naturally into this mode on most occasions when they are unsure of the alternatives.

The examples of writing by more able pupils which I have included illustrate Key Stage 2 children very much in control of their work. They have understood the task they have been given or, in some instances, have set themselves. They have understood the purpose of their writing, recognised the potential audience for these pieces and moved towards a mode of expression which conveys their meaning appropriately. Most of them have been through a number of stages of drafting, the writers confidently and boldly discarding material which was thought to be redundant or distracting, often in discussion with a supportive adult. One of the strengths of all these passages is their economy and tightness. They remain clearly focused. Teachers might well come across such examples in their own classrooms, but they serve as good models of what young people are capable of achieving with a sense of self-belief, and an environment where their work is challenged.

In the example in Figure 6.7 the poet is 7 years old and in Year 3. This amazingly controlled poem maintains its rhythm for all its sixteen lines, but manages, through its accurate and careful punctuation, to be read in a varied manner. Unlike so many rhyming poems by children of the same age, it never sacrifices meaning for the rhyme and the couplets make perfect sense. This poet has a wonderful sense of humour, and uses evocative words ('swishes') to establish accurate description, whilst coining new words ('loggish') to combine rhythmical and descriptive needs. The 'what next?' feature is more difficult with quality material of this sort: I might be asking the poet to look again at the second and penultimate lines. I would certainly be welcoming any further examples of rhyming poetry from this pupil.

The second poem (Figure 6.8), written by another Year 3 pupil, was a direct response to biological study undertaken in class. It is a considerable piece of free verse, with a clear delight in the accurate scientific words ('Stigma, Ovary and Stamens') which have been learned in the study set alongside some powerful imagery ('a root peeps cautiously out','silky as a petticoat'), but there are moments ('many days pass by' and 'it makes a last effort and succeeds in making the flower') when it comes close to resembling prose. The 'what next?' dialogue would be given to exploring a greater consistency of poetic language, achieving the economy which characterises a stronger achievement.

The Crocodile
The terrifying crocodile
Comes waddling down the river Nile.
She's fierce and frightening, muddy, too.
And mean and pasty I'll tell you.
And when she lazes in the sun,
She's cool and damp and never fun.
And when she swishes in the swamp,
She's wickedly waiting for a romp.
To feel, she's scaly, large and long,
Compared with me, she's very strong.
And when she lies within the swamp,
She's muddy, loggish, wet, and damp.
She'd usually give me such a fright,
All creepy, crawling, green and white.
But please don't crawl into her mouth's gap,
Because her jaws just might go SNAP!

Figure 6.7

The Poppy Diary

Oval, smooth seed in the ground,
Damp with the morning dew,
A root peeps cautiously out, then
spreads itself all through the damp
soil,
Next a shoot and two leaves stretch
themselves towards the sun.
Many days pass by, and the stem and
leaves grow
The stem stands to attention, thick
and strong, overloaded with sap.
It makes a last effort and succeeds
In making the flower
Curled, fragile, red petals, silky as
a petticoat,
Stigma, Ovary and Stamens enclosed
inside.
The honey bee comes,
its furry body brushes against the
anthers.
The seeds forming are blown by the
wind,
To find another home.

Figure 6.8

With both poets showing so much insight about the nature of poetic form, it would be helpful to find examples of different sorts of poems, either similar in content to the versions which have been written, or sharing the same subject matter, but dealt with in alternative ways. What able poetry writers really need at this stage is to study other poetry so that they can consider their own attempts alongside it. They also need to be shown, once again, that reading and writing have a close interactive relationship, one constantly setting off aspects of the other.

The next four examples are not related, but are included to show the sorts of range that more able writers have attempted. The first (Figure 6.9), by a 9-year-old girl (who wrote the Key Stage 1 letter in Figure 6.2), was also completely unaided, springing from an idea of her own to compile a 'time capsule' of contemporary artefacts. The second (Figure 6.10) is the script of a talk to her class by a young musician who has recently begun to play the violin. The writer was also 9 years old, in Year 4, and the author of the radio script (Figure 6.5). The same writer was also responsible for the third piece in this section (Figure 6.11), a simple allegorical composition, written a year later. The fourth sample (Figure 6.12), by a slightly older pupil in Year 6, successfully re-tells a well-known story in a wholly original way.

The unusual collection shown in Figure 6.9 is written in the little used reference style. The writer has instinctively absorbed the information about the phonetic assistance necessary to help decode new words ('dijital wotch', 'coyn') from sources such as the dictionary and made an excellent attempt of her own to reproduce that information. The 'definitions' are masterpieces of economy and are stripped to the bare minimum. The whole collection shows a clear understanding of a potential audience, some time in the future, who might stumble across these items, unknown in that time. The 'what next?' factor would involve the wrong use of 'you' in respect of the identity cards, and probably the use of 'we' in this context. The writer is capable of presenting information in this text type in an appropriately detached, distant manner. I would also encourage some more examples, and challenge the writer to give even more information in fewer words!

An actual violin was meant to accompany the talk at Figure 6.10, and there are also moments when music on audio cassette is intended to illustrate points being made. To a great extent it is almost an essay, although there are nods towards a spoken presentation ('Here is a violin played more slowly'). In 'what next?' conversation I would want to encourage the writer to include more phrases in the 'script' which could help to draw the audience into the talk (e.g. 'as you can see'). Nevertheless, this is a well organised set of related ideas, which would lead to an entertaining few minutes of information.

'The Valley of the Rainbows' (Figure 6.11) is a wholly self-possessed piece of work; extremely successful in its own terms. The writer is a very confident story-teller and draws on a wide repertoire of story knowledge. It is a piece which enjoys the richness of its language and expression, and indicates a knowledge of language operating beyond just surface meaning. In the 'what next?' reflection I

DIGITAL WATCH
Pronounced dijital wotch
We use these to tell the time
We strap them on our wrists

COMPUTER CHIP
Pronounced compyewter chip
We put these in special machines
and they store information. The
machines work on electricity.

IDENTITY CARDS.
Pronounced: eye-dent-itey cards
The card on the left shows you belong
to a club, the card on the right is to show
us who you are and the passport lets you
into other countries

COIN
Pronounced coyn
We use these to trade with.
We give people coins and they give us
something in return.
The face on the coin is the Queen's

Figure 6.9

THE VIOLIN

The violin has four strings : G, D, A and E. It makes approximately 44 notes. It is the smallest and highest pitched member of the string family.

There are two ways of playing the violin: bowing or plucking, which is called Pizzicato. Pizzicato playing is done by the second or index finger of the right hand touching any string.Bowing is done by moving the bow across the strings so that they vibrate.

When the bow is pulled across the strings or the finger plucks the strings the sound goes through the bridge and into the hollow body where it is amplified.The sound returns through the sound holes and makes the noise that is heard when somebody plays the violin.The violin can make different sounds. It can go slow or fast. Here is a violin played fast.(PLAY TAPE HERE) Here is a violin played more slowly.(PLAY TAPE HERE)

In an orchestra the violinists sit on either side of the conductor.The first violin, in line with the conductor, is the leader of the orchestra.

People need to be skilful with their hands to make violins and sometimes it takes months to make one good violin.They are mostly hand-made. As a result violins are expensive and most people borrow one until they are sure that they really do want to learn to play!

To make a violin a flat surface of dyed maple wood is needed to carve out the body. It is then smoothed out and the process is repeated for the other side of the violin. Another piece of maple is then needed to join the two together. The upper piece of carved maple has two 'f' shaped holes in it. A piece of metal about 9 centimetres long is fixed on to the wood below these holes.
The fingerboard is made of ebony and attached to the neck and scroll which are also made of maple.The neck and scroll has four holes drilled in it for the tuning pegs.This entire section is then attached to the body and the violin starts to take shape.
The tailpiece is carved and put on, as is the endpin. The chinrest is screwed on next. The tuning pegs are fitted in and the strings put on.Lastly the bridge is wedged in, the whole violin varnished and the violin is ready to play.

For the bow, a long stick of wood wider at the bottom than at the top is prepared.Horse hair is gathered into a tidy bundle and a piece of metal is threaded on to flatten them out.A rectangular piece of wood with a curve for the thumb called the frog is put onto the stick and the horsehair is secured at both ends.The screw to adjust the bow is fastened on last.

Figure 6.10

The Valley of the Rainbows

The world in which Janey lived was entirely black and white. The black trees stood out against the sombre, grey sky. The people had white skins and prominent black features. They were tiresome and dull people, with spiky hair and black clothes. Janey was a black and white person and was always bored or miserable. What could possibly cheer her up in a black bedroom? She was tired of eating white cereal and black toast on black and white crockery every morning.

One morning, Janey was walking to school, under the wintry sky and tramping through the white leaves, when, in a little thicket, she came upon a bird she had never seen before. It had green feathers, a red beak, blue feet and a yellow plume. Janey's surprise at seeing such a colourful bird in a colourless land, like hers, was extreme. She hesitantly approached the bird to ask from where it came. Its reply told her of a land called The Valley of the Rainbows that boasted every colour imaginable.

Janey begged the bird to take her there, which it willingly did. It flew over the black hills and black trees and, finally, over a white wall. It landed on the other side, in the Valley of the Rainbows. Janey was dazzled by the colours. All around her were ripe green fruit, dangling from sturdy brown trees, red brick houses with purple curtains in their windows. Yellow flowers covered the hillside and, above the valley, shone a glittering sun in the blue sky. The people wore clothes of all the colours of the rainbow and carried paintbrushes and palettes from which they enlivened any possibility of a dull world.

Janey wished her world resembled this kaleidoscope of colours. While she was reflecting on this idea, she saw a paintbox that had apparently been abandoned. She stuffed it into her pocket and asked the bird to take her back to her black and white world, which it did obediently. There, she took out the paintbrush and dipped it into the green paint. As Janey painted the sky, the whole world turned green! The skin of all the people was a peculiar lime-green, and felt clammy, like frogs' skin. Their hair was a dirty bottle-green, and their clothes were different shades of fluorescent green. They appeared dirty, but were calm and peaceful in nature. The trees were beautiful dark greens and all the rivers were sea greens, but none of the colours resembled the beauty of the Valley of the Rainbows, with the sky and the sun just sickly shades of green.

In a panic, Janey feverishly sought out the coloured bird. It was found pecking at a green insect by a green river. She pleaded with it to tell her what to do. The bird replied that Janey was not using the paintbox correctly, as the people in the Valley had done, and that she must carefully mix the paints before separately painting each thing in her world with great care. Janey fetched the paintbox and asked the bird to show her. The bird mixed a shade of light peach, then with careful strokes dabbed at the worm in which it was interested. Slowly, the green faded and turned to a soft pink colour. Janey saw how simple the process was and resolved to use her new skills to transform the world and fulfil her dreams.

Figure 6.11

would want to consider how the contrast of the two parts of the story might be made even stronger, and look again at the end, which is not fully developed. I would also ask the writer to think of some real life situations which might be given a different perspective by being considered in this manner.

In Figure 6.12, this writer has learned an impressive number of story-telling conventions, and knows how to produce a piece of narrative with power and pace. She enjoys showing off her language prowess ('bidding Red Riding Hood be quiet until she heard her cue', 'Grandma faked a sigh', and 'stepped back, coughed three times, rolled his eyes and fell backwards on the floor') and the organisation of the story is tightly controlled. There are moments of awkwardness ('Wolfie, being a simple wolf, not given to seeing through tricky plots, took this as he was meant to ... ' and too many uses of 'then' in paragraph six), which would be part of the 'what next?' discussion. I am also not absolutely sure of the plot in the early stages, and would wish to see clearer motivation for Grandma's intentions. I would certainly want to look afresh at another tale with this writer, possibly from another unusual narrative position, perhaps like that of the wolf in Jon Sziescka's *The True Story of the 3 Little Pigs*.

Pupils almost routinely make responses to research tasks through narrative forms, unless they are directed otherwise. Most of the pieces of prose in Figures 6.13–6.17 have been written as a consequence of classroom-based study, or because personal interest has motivated further reading and finding out. More able writers can often be identified by their willingness to want to share their extended ideas, in a manner which conveys the excitement and enthusiasm they have felt during their research. These pieces of writing are good illustrations of that enjoyment, even where the subject matter is sometimes gloomy. The first two examples are by different Year 6 boys, from different schools, in response to drama based situations. The letter resulted from a study of correspondence home from the First World War trenches; the other piece from watching a presentation by other pupils of the Plague at Eyam in Derbyshire.

The writer at Figure 6.13 has tried to move in under the skin of the character he is representing: a young man from a less than grand background, caught up in the rhetoric and glamour of war. I would be interested in discussing with the pupil the contrasts in the letter, and what they might convey about the thoughts of the character concerned.

The example at Figure 6.14 is an extraordinarily moving and vivid piece of work; this topic has really touched the writer. It comprises a confident flashback contained within a carefully structured descriptive narrative. There are some organisational matters which I would be pleased to discuss with the writer, but little else which might be relevant or helpful in this context!

The next three examples are by the same girl, the first piece written when in Year 4, the other two produced when in Year 5. They illustrate a real progression in her development. The first of her pieces (Figure 6.15), written after reading *Carrie's War* by Nina Bawden and *Goodnight Mr Tom* by Michelle Magorian,

Red Riding Hood

An Alternative Version

Once upon a time there lived a young wolf named Wolfie. One day Wolfie woke up from a midday snooze feeling very hungry, in fact he felt excessively hungry, and lo and behold, when he got up and looked in his larder, the shelves were bare. 'Oh well!', he thought, and looked in his piggy bank. The was nothing there, Wolfie was broke! He went outside and sat down to think.

A few minutes later there was a loud roar and an old Grandma rode by on a motor bike. She saw Wolfie and Wolfie saw her, and already a plan was forming in her clever mind. Quickly Grandma put on the brakes and hopped off the bike. Miserably, Wolfie looked up at her as she advanced towards him. "Hungry" he whimpered. That fitted in excellently with Grandma's plan.

"Well then", she grinned, "You'd best come back with me, I've got my grandaughter coming over today." Wolfie, being a simple wolf, not given to seeing through tricky plots, took this as he was meant to, and, coming to the conclusion that Grandma wasn't very clever, he decided that, when a suitable time arose, he could quite easily eat the pair of them, he nodded and followed the motorbike as it zoomed home towards the little cottage.

Parking the bike on the path, Grandma undid both Yale locks and hurried in to switch off the burglar alarm. Wolfie, puzzled, followed her, and she led him into the sitting room. "Now, you just

Figure 6.12

sit there quietly," Grandma indicated a comfy chair, from which the front door could not be seen. "and I will go and fetch my grandaughter, Red Riding Hood." Wolfie sat down with a sigh and began to plan how it would be best to devour Grandma and Red Riding Hood when they returned. He had not got very far however, when he fell asleep.

Meanwhile, Grandma was speeding to the other side of the wood. Once there she collected not only Red Riding Hood but also a fresh set of Red Riding Hood's clothes. When they returned Grandma took a peek through the window and, seeing Wolfie fast asleep, she knew they had plenty of time.

She took Red Riding Hood quietly upstairs and together they manouvered the old dress makers dummy into the wardrobe. Then Red Riding Hood took off her cape, with it's red hood, and wriggled under Grandma's bed. Grandma then hastily dressed the dummy in the spare clothes and the red cape, pulling the hood up so that it looked like a person with their back to you. Then, bidding Red Riding Hood be quiet until she heard her cue, she clattered downstairs, making as much noise as possible, and entered the sitting room.

Wolfie, woken by the clattering, was just stretching himself. "Wolfie" said Grandma, very sweetly. "Red Riding Hood has seen you through the window, and was so frightened that she has run upstairs and hidden in my wardrobe. To persuade her to come out you will have to show her what a nice wolf you are really." She led the way up stairs

Figure 6.12 continued

and Wolfie followed her thinking, 'Ah ha! How perfect, it will be easy now to make a meal of the stupid twit and her Grandma!'

"Come on Red Riding Hood" said Grandma, opening the wardrobe door. "Not coming out" said Red Riding Hood. "Wolfie is very nice" said Grandma persuasively, "No!" said Red Riding Hood stubbornly, from under the bed. Grandma faked a sigh and said, "Wolfie, I hand over to you." She stepped aside and sat on the bed.

With a roar, Wolfie leapt at the dummy and sunk his teeth into it. The sawdust poured out and filled his throat, choking him. He stepped back, coughed three times, rolled his eyes and fell backward on the floor.

Red Riding Hood came out from under the bed. "Wow!" she said. Together, she and Grandma dragged Wolfie down, out of the house and int the wood, where they left him to recover. Then they both went home for tea and lived happily ever after. For Wolfie never went near a human again!

Figure 6.12 continued

```
Josh

  Friend and little brother. I'm on the ferry over to France at
the moment. It's taking longer than I thought. We are in for a
nasty storm the Captain said. Already the sea is starting to
sway beneath us. Dark swelling storm clouds quietly pursue us
across a watery plain. We have already been told to go below.
We do so with no objection, no one wanting to be caught in the
downpour soon to come. The sea is getting worse. The waves start
to lash the bow like a wild animal trying to force its way into
the ship. Back and forth we rock, a cork in a plethora of
turbulance, but does this fierce weather bother us? Nay, not us.
A hardy breed of men we are, with hair on our chests and
unshaven faces. Guns at our sides, we sing old sea chanties and
cheer. Filled to the brim with beer and glee, slapping each
other on the back for battles yet to be won and sparring with
shadows of foe not yet seen. The tired or withdrawn compromising
with polishing their rifles with such loving care, but with such
a    silent    solitude.    Knowing    that    these    fine    works    of
craftmanship, with gleaming barrels and varnished wooden handles
might one day soon have to go against all we think moral and
holy. In the brief they gave earler there was one motto that
was drummed into our minds, "Kill or be killed!" And now some
sit pondering the options. I dearly hope that I will not have
to take a life, no matter how evil it is made out to be,

                                Love,
                                Tom
```

Figure 6.13

followed by some further research in memories of evacuation collected by Ben Wicks, is a series of imagined situations of an evacuee. The content is important to the writer, and she wants to include as much of her knowledge about the time as she can. All the different little scenes, each of which could be developed separately, are superficially dealt with. In the second piece (Figure 6.16), the research is still important, but a more convincing character has been devised through which to convey what has been discovered about contemporary life for these people. The two purposes of the writing hang together more successfully. The final example (Figure 6.17) in this section is the most mature of them all. The writer has begun to realise that the story and the characters can be secondary to exploring the business of writing itself. She was tired of yet another 'first person' 'being there' exercise, which she can clearly manage. After a little preliminary discussion with an adult, the writer decided to attempt to explore whether she could spread the narrative centre through different sorts of text type.

ALONE:

He knelt down upon the tough stoney soil of the graveyard, hands clasped before him. A small roughly hewn wooden cross, lashed together at the centre, lay imbeded in the newly dug grave. "I've buried my only son here with my bare hands" He thought bitterly. Gradually he began to recite the words of prayer.

> O Father, my lord,
> take this soul to you,
> and may you grant the
> great gift of eternal
> life in your kingdom.
> Amen

Slowly he began to rise, facing the church of his home village. Its ornately carved tower stretched up to meet the sky. "I'm sorry" He whispered as the waining sun began to set. The horizon was streaked with all manners of reds and yellows, merging together to form one spectacular display. "Life is cruel" He wondered. It was time to remember, and to recollect.

"Mummy" A young boy stepped solomly forward. His sharp face was concealed in a matted mess of brown hair, but it was clear that he had been crying. "Mummy, what's wrong, why are they doing this?" The woman lifted her head and turned towards him. Her eyes were filled with desperation. "No, please don't" She moaned softly in a barely audible voice. He knew she was not addressing him.
"Move boy" Rasped a voice from behind. A figure dressed in long heavy Clerical robes pushed by, and knelt beside her. "Take the boy away, he should not witness this" Heavy hands clasped him, and he felt, as if in a dream, being pulled away. From inside the small wooden shack the clerk began to read a prayer. "Lord, may you cleanse this unclean soul with the fire of your wrath, for this woman has worshiped the Devil itself. She is no longer fit to live, but instead consumed by the flames of hell..." The terrible incantation continued, flowing over the weakly struggling child like a drowsy shroud. He was dragged back firmly, out of the door and into the rippling fields of corn outside. The following silence was split by a cry of pain. With his last remaining strength he turned his head. His home stood, consumed my dancing flames that licked at its edges like

Figure 6.14

a hungry beast. Lingering shadows stood by watching, silent until now. Slowly a solomn chant was taken up, resounding through his head. "Witch, witch, witch, witch" It continued. He could remember no more.

"Witch, witch, witch.." The words haunted him, taunting, frustrating. The first loss in his life of grief. Thinking back on past experiences he remembered the death of his wife and son, the only people left dear to him. Once again he was alone.

"God has chosen our punishment, the world is doomed!" He turned to the source of the sound, stopping for one moment.

Two men, clothed in white simple garb, stood in one corner of the bustling village square, around which a perplexed and interested crowd had gathered. "It will take us all, hunt us down wherever we sleep, wherever we hide. Praise the Lord, for this is the last chance to show your fealty. The black death is among us even as we speak, an illness to cleanse the world of all that is wrong and foul!" Silence fell for one moment as the figure composed himself, before he continued. "We have all sinned terribly and deserve to die" As he said this he produced a short leather lash from around his waist, displaying it to the entranced crowd. "He has sinned!" The man cried, bringing the whip down upon his partner's unprotected back. Moaning softly he fell forward on to his knees, mumbling something under his breath. "We have sinned!"

Disgusted he turned away, continuing on his journey through the dirty streets, littered with rubbish and rotting debris. Shortly afterwards he halted in a narrow back street, staring up at one thatched building towering above him. His home. He noticed with trepidation that the door lay open, swinging slightly in the soft breeze. As he stepped inside he fell to his knees with shock. Before him lay the body of a woman his wife, cradling a small infant lovingly. Neither moved.

And so he had suffered, his Mother, Wife and Son had left him, alone here in this cruel world. It was wrong some how, it should have been him, not them. Slowly, reluctantly he turned away, leaving his past life, starting anew. He had not noticed it, but a single tear coursed down his face to splash against the ground below.

Figure 6.14 continued

The diary and letter forms meant that she could still move into the security of the first person on occasions, but wrapped in areas of further challenge. The school history book and the newspaper presented further challenges, requiring further research to discover suitable 'models'. Probably the least successful section is that of *The Daily Border*, and this would be the topic of further 'what next?' evaluation.

Key Stage 3

Teachers of pupils who are identified as more able writers in Key Stage 3 should look through the examples already discussed, to see what their younger counterparts are capable of producing. I have not included examples of older writers because of problems of space, but the examples of younger pupils should offer sufficient evidence that the highest expectations can be made of their work.

All pupils in Years 7 to 9 should be able to articulate their intentions about their writing before they pick up a pen, if their earlier preparation has been properly planned and progressive. In that context the better writers will be using the writing process to *explore* the possibilities of making their meanings in the most significant ways. The example in Figure 6.17 shows how a writer can take enormous responsibility and control for her own work; she was not content with an approach already satisfactorily practised, and wanted to look at further possibilities. Similar opportunities should be available for others displaying the same skills. If this way of working is not familiar, then a new culture will need to be created.

For many pupils the customary devices of reading a text and then writing a personal response, very often in the style of a diary entry or letter, to indicate their level of 'comprehension' and insight, is perfectly valid. Their own progression as writers might need further challenge and support to develop in such tasks. For more assured writers who have already shown their competence in these contexts, however, there is a far wider repertoire of possible text types they should be encountering, deconstructing and replicating. Teachers should be expecting these pupils to act like writers, who have a clear sense of the ways they are moving and having effects on their audiences. If, as so often happens in classrooms at this stage, pupils are asked to write an 'autobiography', the more able should be familiar with a range of autobiographical approaches, from which to choose their own preferred style, or they may opt for something original. I have read hundreds of 'autobiographies' by pupils at this age, most of which have not been modelled on examples which are intended to tell more about their subjects through the style. Similarly, it is not unusual to see pupils being set writing tasks in the form of newspaper articles. While many of these pieces begin satisfactorily, few are sustained and virtually none are closely modelled on recognisable tabloid or broadsheet examples. More able writers should be achieving that closer resemblance to the original.

Chapter 1. The Journey

My brother was 4 and I was 9 when the war started on Sunday the 3rd September, 1939. The air-raid siren went when we were in church, and we all ran out but it was a false alarm. Mother kept saying, "Don't worry, Jean, it'll be alright." but I was still frightened.

My name is Jean Helk, and I was evacuated from London on 11th September 1939 to Ilfracombe in North Devon. We were sent home on the evening of September 10th with a letter to tell us to bring a suitcase packed with a change of clothes, a packed lunch, a toilet bag and our gas-mask. We gathered at the school and had a label fastened to each of us. Next, we were faced with a half-hour walk to the station. My gas-mask kept banging (and bruising) my leg, and my brother, Brian, kept whining about his legs aching. After what seemed decades, we arrived at the station. We were piled on to the trains waving to weeping mothers and fathers. There was a four-hour ride on the hot, stuffy train, during which my brother complained of missing home, so I gave him my lunch. The train was filled with sick and urine by the time we reached our destination.

Chapter 2

I got out of the train with my brother. We were taken to a town hall in silence.
"I think there's going to be a party," whispered Brian. "Shut-up" I hissed, and received a fierce look from Miss Hunt, my teacher. As all one hundred of us filed into the room we saw rows of women. I think there must have been about 50 of them. When we were all in we made a semi-circle and the women drifted round, looking at us.

I was one of the last to be picked, what with my brother crying and us looking so dishevelled. Eventually, I was taken round with a Billeting Officer. The people who finally accepted us owned a butcher's shop. We were given a meal and as it was 8.30 we were put straight to bed.

Chapter 3

The people we stayed with were a middle-aged couple, with a daughter called Flo. The woman was small, with her long brown hair tied up, so that she did not trip over it. She had snappy blue eyes, a puckered mouth and steel-rimmed spectacles. The man of the house was a butcher, so every morning we would see him striding down the stairs in his blue and white apron and big brown shoes. I loved meat and this seemed to please him.

I quickly made friends with Flora. She taught me how to pick berries and recognise flowers and trees. Sometimes our foster father let us help in the shop. Alas this bliss was not last long.

Figure 6.15

Now, our foster parents had not got an indoor toilet and my brother, Brian, kept wetting his bed. This could be coped with and the sheets could be washed, but one night he could not bear the dark, and he was too scared to go down to the toilet, so he used his bed not only for urine but also his excrement! The damage was done and the next morning we were rushed straight round to the Billeting Officer, as fast as our legs would carry us.

Chapter 4

At three o'clock that afternoon, we eventually found our second home, with a large, muscular woman called Mrs Bite. Her husband was away fighting in France. She was a hideous woman. She had a son of her own, whom she regularly petted.

We had to get up at 5 o'clock every morning to light the stove, prepare the oxo and fetch the milk. When these jobs had been done we had to trudge up a hill with a large bucket, to the village water pump and fetch the water for Mrs Bite's tea and the oxo. After school (Mrs Bite came back from visiting at about 5.30) I had to do all the cleaning of the house and make the tea. If these jobs were not done (they usually were not to Mrs Bite's satisfaction) I was boxed on the ears or beaten more severely.

I got no breakfast, lunch was served at school and tea was bread and water or oxo. I lived in these conditions for six months, along with my brother. Eventually we devised a plan. We knew that Mrs Bite always looked at our letters to our parents, before sealing and stamping them. We wrote in our letters how nasty our foster mother was, and how she starved us. It did the trick! The next afternoon we came home to find our baggage on the front door step.

Chapter 5

We were reported to be children with a bad reputation, so me and an ugly girl, with a squint, were taken to a children's home. We stayed for nearly two years. I think there were about 200 children living there, meals were slight, being mostly tinned food, powdered milk and eggs and dried potatoes. We wore the same clothes for a whole week. But, in spite of these difficulties we managed to make friends and be generally satisfied.

On January 5th 1942 we received a letter from our mother saying that she intended to move to a small place in Scotland called Kirkudbright. She enclosed the train tickets and said that she was looking forward to us joining her.

My evacuation days were over at last.

Figure 6.15 continued

Our Life on a Barge

From the moment of my birth, I have lived on a barge. My family have lived on barges for decades. My mother named me William, after the barge, because I was born exactly ten years after the barge was built.

I recall spending time talking or babbling to Flissie, my older sister, whilst being tied to the top of the barge, as no adults could spare time to give me attention. It was the safest place to be, and everyone knew where to find me. At five I was expected to help on the boat. I would groom the horse or help to push lock gates, or shop and run other errands. When I was six, my little sister Sadie was born and Flissie had to look after her too.

Our barge was small and cramped, but very cosy. It was always filled with lots of small items, such as plates with laced edges and brass articles. The range was black and shiny, and took up much of the central space. Our beds were very small and built against the side of the barge. All the babies would sleep in a box, because of the lack of space. At meal times, a table would be let down from the wall which we all sat around. A dimly lit oil lamp was the only form of illumination. Everywhere was adorned with paint, especially roses and castles. Food was fish, sheep, fowl or eggs, sometimes stolen from canal-side farms. Father would catch fish occasionally, and manage a little poaching where he could. I was quite scruffily dressed in cast-off clothes, which were washed in the canal water, as was our shared potty! I did not wash much either, as valuable fresh water was kept to drink.

I seem to remember members of our family being frequently ill, for stuffy cabins brought on chest wheezes and streaming eyes. I can remember wheezing in the stuffy cabin but later, when put outside I caught a chill and had a high temperature in the cold air. I also remember knocking over a kettle and scalding part of my arm. I was tended to with a cold towel and water, and scolded for wasting the water, for it was nearly half a kettleful!

A visit to the doctor was impossible, and putting our feet up in hospital meant being minus a day's wages; so we would have early bedtime and firmer wrapping up, or longer in the fresh air if we were ill. If we hurt ourselves, we would have a cardboard splint on. One cold, icy morning Father went to begin walking the horse. We heard Father bellow and roar as he slipped on the ice on the towpath. He fell into the canal and as he gripped the ropes, they made the horse panic and it fell in too. The horse pushed Father down again and again as it thrashed around. We pulled Father out with a stick, but he had broken four bones and was cut all over. The horse was crushed between the barge and canal wall when it swung round, and died three hours later. Whilst I was helping I was sick with the shock of the event.

It was important that all the family were available to work, and took their full part in the jobs to be done, as we all had to give as much effort as possible. Our pay depended on getting our cargo to its destination quickly. This was made worse by knowing that more and more goods were being moved by the new railways. They were being built in all parts of the country and we saw their smoke and steam from the canal with increasing despair and alarm.

Our boat transported coal around Britain. It was not the worst cargo, although it was still dirty and heavy work. There were boats which carried all sorts of unhealthy loads, including manure, which would often cause disease and make the whole living area stink. We still had to put up with rats and other vermin.

My sister Flissie often had to do grown women's work. She would do the washing and cooking with mother, and usually tended to the little ones. At one time mother became a little sickly, and Flissie was relied upon for all the cooking and cleaning. Jobs like sewing and cooking would be

Figure 6.16

done on the move. She also helped with the loading and unloading wherever that was needed. It was a common sight to see the women shovelling coal into sacks and working the winches to lift great loads ashore. We would all have to cart the loads of coal out of the butty and add them to the pile. That could take up to three hours. Another job, which I shared with my sister Sadie, was that of mooring at the coal wharfs. We would each drag a piece of black work-worn rope on to the shore. We would tie the rope in hard knots to the rotten mooring posts. Tying knots was another skill we had to learn. We were always glad to get back to the boat to moor upstream for the night, but before I could sleep I would look the horse over and settle it for the night.

I would groom the horse three times a week and take it for rides. We had strong old horses, one of which bore the name of Henery. These animals would have the strength of eleven men. The horses often got more attention than ourselves, although some barge people drove their animals very hard, and did not let them rest. Our horse drank and ate from a painted bowl. A crocheted piece of material draped over its ears kept off the flies. Its reins were covered with brasses. I would have to stable it for the night. The best job was walking the horse over the hill at the tunnels, which might sometimes mean walking miles.

It was certainly much better than "legging", which I recall particularly clearly. I can see now the dark, dirty tunnels through which father and I legged boats. This was achieved by us both lying on our backs, on a plank sticking out from the boat, and pressing our feet to the tunnel walls, to "walk" the boat through. The water and dirt dripped from the roof and made it extra unpleasant for us. Almost as difficult was the job of steering the boat, especially with other barges shoving their way to the front of queues at places like locks and wharfs.

I did not socialise much with people on the land, as they regarded our dirty bodies and filthy clothes with distaste, as well as thinking of our fathers as being drunkards and other nasty things. But as a small boy I would like to see other barge boys, when I had a chance. I did have a few friends who I saw at odd times. Boys of my own age such as Trevor, Colin, Martin, Hubie, Bert and Robert I was able to talk to for short intervals. As a family, our only excuses for socializing would be at weddings, christenings, and funerals, when we all got together and had a good time.

There was no education for the canal children, although I slowly learned to read bridge and town names, even though I often read them wrongly. We were happy to let Napton be "Nopton" and Barnton be "Burnton", for there was no one to put us right.

In recent times the most prominent event of my life has happened. This was my 25th birthday, when I had saved enough for my own barge. Three days later, Father and I travelled on foot to a wharf, to buy a boat. As I had no wife or children, a small, cheap barge was bought. It was a four berth.

That very day, I went back to our barge with a heavy heart. Flissie was married already, but I bid my goodbyes to the rest of the family. I remember Mother's hug and kiss very well, and the way she cried as I walked to my own barge.

And so at the end of my diaries, I walk along, steering my horse who steers my barge. I observe my apprentice, and think of myself at 11, Father teaching me about the barge. I reflect upon my early life, and my family. I then realised fully that I was on my own. When I entered the barge that night I looked round admiringly at the iron pans and plates that I had been given by Mother. There, waiting for me was the apprentice. I was sailing into what I knew would be an uncertain future.

Figure 6.16 continued

Diary of Petra Carrson
14th March 1595

Rumour has it that the reivers are coming soon! I go all shivery as I write the words. A neighbouring farmer galloped over to tell us this morning. When Mother heard, she covered her face with her hands and ran from the table, crying. I started to shake and Papa held me on his lap like he did when I was little. When I had eventually calmed down, he told me to fetch some milk from the dairy. I did but when I was walking back, I heard a distressed servant shouting, "They'll be heere tomorra neet!" and gasps from the listeners. As I heard this my knees collapsed beneath me, I heard the thud as my head hit the floor and everything went black.

A School History Book

During the years 1500 to 1650, terrible robbing gangs roamed the border country between England and Scotland. They were called Reivers. They attacked or reived houses and stole food, clothes and animals. Several stories exist today about their frightening activities. One well-known raid was when the Carrson house was attacked. The reivers set the Carrson house on fire and stole everything of value. Then, when the grandfather Armstrong attempted to stop them, he was shot. The rest of the family then escaped to Tullie House in Carlisle where they lived for six months, before moving to and settling in Manchester. A museum can be found in Carlisle today in Mr James Tullie's name. If you are ever in the area, you may want to to discover more about these events.

Tullie House
Carlisle
Cumberland

31st March 1595

My dearest Margaret

I write to you in deepest sorrow. As you will gather from the address, we are lodging at Tullie House, the reason being that not long ago the reivers (I shudder to write this) destroyed our house by fire. Before they came (we heard news of their coming) we managed to pack a few necessities and flee.

But then the Reivers arrived! They sang a victory song and set our great house and the surrounding buildings alight with blazing torches. We were terrified and paralysed by their power.

Poor Papa. He was killed in the most cowardly way, when he staggered out of the burning house. He threatened the Reivers with swords, but they shot him with muskets. I sobbed and shrieked over Papa and covered myself with his blood when I sat him up and hugged him. I placed his granddaughter, Clara, in his arms and shouted curses at the Reivers. Then I escaped into the dark night with Peter and the children.

The rest of us struggled on, through bad weather, especially very fierce storms. The children were constantly frightened and Clara contracted fever, poor thing. She nearly died of choking, as we cowered in a hedge. After two weeks of struggle, we had entered the town of Carlisle and were taken in by an old friend, a kind man by name of Mr James Tullie. We are now living in his happy home. It is our intention to escape the border area.

Yours dearly
Anne

Figure 6.17

THE DAILY BORDER

Carrson Home Destroyed in Raid

Late on the night of 13th March, the Carrson house was attacked by Reivers. Apparently, according to the mother, Mrs Anne Carrson, they approached on horseback at the dead of night.

The grandfather, Osbert Armstrong, was shot dead when trying to halt the evil deeds of the attacking reivers. The reivers stole horses, cattle, food, money and jewellery. They burnt the house to the ground and then left at approximately two o'clock.

The rest of the family are currently lodged at Mr James Tullie's house in Carlisle, to which they escaped on that fateful night. No one else was hurt, but Anne Carson's two year old daughter, Clara, has a severe fever. The whole family are suffering from severe shock.

The Carrson and Armstrong families are respected ones in this area, especially Osbert Armstrong who lived in his house for eighty four years. The family was joined to the Carrsons when Peter Carrson married Anne Armstrong, as reported in this journal 14 years ago. The house was an extensive one, richly appointed, with many servants, but it has suffered cruelly from the fire deliberately caused by the murderous intruders. Sadly, it now stands ruined and derelict. Since the disaster the family have been trying to plan settling down to normal family life in another part of England.

Diary of Petra Carrson

10th October 1595

I am writing this diary entry in the nursery that I share with Clara in our new home in Manchester. On 21st September, we left Tullie House and started our journey to the new house that Papa has bought. Glory be! Tonight I can go to bed and feel secure in the knowledge that I can sleep until the morning sun shines on my face. Today I went to fetch milk. I spent the whole journey enjoying the safety of the town. Tomorrow I shall get out of bed and rush outside and greet the morning and my new life that awaits me.

Figure 6.17 continued

As a final idea in this section I would like to suggest that teachers can assist all writers more closely if they have an understanding about the stages of writing growth *within* different text types. The English departments at Lord Williams's School, Thame, and Didcot Girls' School had begun to articulate for themselves the different levels of, for example, 'discursive writing' or 'narrative writing', with the associated responsibility for teaching pupils those types of texts, in the same way their primary colleagues had begun exploring (Figure 4.3, p.41). These initiatives have meant a subsequent closer attention to writing in different genres, and the best texts to read and study to support all pupils in their clearer understanding of what is being asked of them. Writing for all these pupils is much less stressful and intimidating, and – in circumstances where pupils are more confident about what they could be achieving, and where their control is growing – can be a real source of pleasure.

Chapter 7

More Able Language Users Learning from Texts other than Books

Having identified the more able users of language and given them challenges beyond the ordinary, some teachers can still have difficulty in providing tasks beyond the mainstream reading and writing curriculum. The next few pages contain a number of examples of other forms of text which will extend the understanding of pupils, and allow them to use their skills in related but wider contexts.

Video texts – film and television

Children of all abilities have no difficulty watching video texts! Too often, the parents of more able readers think that their children are wasting their time engaging in such an 'easy' pastime. This belief is completely wrong; children need to know what is happening in video texts, to take the fullest possible meanings from them, exactly as they need to do from book texts. The relationship between book texts and video texts is also very close. A large number of video texts for children are based on book texts, and where they are originally devised for video they have narrative, plot and character features very much in common. To invest time and effort in studying video texts, particularly those based on book texts, is to open up the strong possibility of developing even greater understanding of the book text. It is not unusual for pupils to read a book because they have enjoyed seeing a version of it on television or video.

An example that I know works successfully with young children, especially able young children, is the combined study of John Burningham's book *Grandpa* with the video of the same name, based on the book, made by TVS and Channel 4. Having read through the book and talked about the areas of meaning it conveys, children might be asked to consider what the problems facing a director of a video of the book are likely to be. They will realise that there are not sufficient illustrations in the book to sustain a film of any length. They will also quickly see that the 'flashes' of scenes witnessed in the book will have to be extended to make an animated film interesting; so they have to flesh out the details of the book. They come to see that it will be necessary to give 'grandpa' and his grand daughter 'voices' on the soundtrack; resulting in healthy discussion about the sort of voices which will be required to interpret their characters. Somebody will suggest that music will have to be included, to help establish mood. Further discussion will ensue about types of music, where it will be included and the sorts of sounds which best suit the text. All these areas of discussion and heightened awareness will contribute to the reader's greater understanding of the book text, as well as contributing to that child's further insights into video texts. After all this work, it would be a reasonable reward to allow the pupils to watch the video! All the predictions and suppositions will have to be checked, anyway.

As pupils grow older they can be asked to undertake more sophisticated and demanding comparative studies. They might be asked to think about the plot structures of animated/cartoon programmes most will watch on television as a matter of course in their home viewing. It will not be long before more able children are drawing their own conclusions about the programmes they have not yet seen, which could be recorded by the teacher or the child, for prediction purposes. They are also likely to make associations between stories they are reading and those they are watching, even though they might appear to be unrelated.

The Disney Corporation has achieved its fortune by adapting traditional tales into animated form, and most of these films are now available in video. They give us tremendous insight into the ways that stories always convey important features of their times and cultures. It would be a worthwhile study for children of all ages to consider certain issues within Disney films over the years: the treatment of women and girls, for instance, in films like *Snow White* and *Beauty and the Beast*, made in very different periods, or the differing technologies available to the makers of *Cinderella* and *Toy Story*, or the difference of pace and imagery in *Bambi* and *Aladdin*. Young children will be able to make serious comparative insights when given these sorts of tasks.

The explosion of video distribution has meant that it is now possible to see different productions of television or film versions of book texts, alongside the original text itself. Frances Hodgson Burnett's book *The Secret Garden* would be a good example of a 'three way' study. A modern film, made for the international market, gives a strong contrast with a British television version filmed in the early 1980s, before both of those texts are considered against the book. Has all the detail of the book been included in both filmed versions, and if there are omissions where do they occur? Do the changes affect any aspects of meaning? Are all the same characters in all three texts? Which of the texts is most convincing?

As pupils grow older, so there are selections of more testing texts which lend themselves to similar further study. *Lord of the Flies*, for instance, is a text older readers might enjoy reading and studying in its two – utterly different – film editions. One of the most exciting texts for studying in this way is Shakespeare's

Romeo and Juliet. Teachers will be very grateful to see Baz Luhrmann's recent film version of the play, in complete contrast to Zeffirelli's 1960's interpretation. These two productions so effectively illustrate how audiences in different times make sense of Shakespeare's work. Neither text could have been made in the time of the other, but young people need to be able to work out what that statement means for themselves.

Then there are texts which appear in more than one medium. Terry Pratchett's *Truckers* is a popular book, an animated video and a set of audio cassette readings by Tony Robinson. Pupils could be given experience of all three, making an excellent homework task! Following these readings, viewings and listenings, children can be given a number of comparative questions, allowing them to make greater meaning of all three texts.

Children should also be given opportunities for making video, television or film – and working out some of the differences between the forms of those texts – even if they cannot physically have access to the equipment itself. As could be seen from the *Grandpa* assignment mentioned earlier, it is not necessary to be technically proficient or to have expensive resources available to know some of, and articulate, the issues which affect the makers of those media. Scripting, musical backgrounds and soundtracks, casting decisions and editing matters are all areas in which pupils will be able to show their prowess, and use their knowledge to make further meaning about book and other texts. There are, however, strong and durable video cameras now used more frequently in classrooms, which do allow pupils to see the direct visual representation of their ideas. They will also find out quite quickly that video production is not the same as television or film-making, and perhaps respect television and film production more as a result.

Keeping an eye on current television and film versions of books known to the children is also a potential area of further study for the more able readers. They could be given the task of finding out as many cross-references as they can to book and film or television, to see how the pre-production publicity is presented and to follow up the product 'tie ins' which result from skilful marketing. Teachers who are unaware of the remarkable support materials produced, free of charge, by Film Education (Alhambra House, 27–31 Charing Cross Road, London WC2H 0AU) should contact them to be included on the mailing list. Much of what arrives at your school from this source would be suitable for individual and supported study by more able readers.

Radio

Radio is probably the most underrated and under used broadcast medium. It is cheap and simple to produce in the classroom and can stretch the imagination more than most camera operators will ever conceive. I believe it is possible to sink the *Titanic* on radio in any classroom, but it would be impossible to film there! With some very simple sound effects, always possible to make, a whole world of experience is within the grasp of the broadcaster. There are many available models on which to base radio productions which children are capable of making.

Even if young children are not as accustomed to listening to drama as they are to viewing it, it will not take many attempts at the form before they begin coming to their own conclusions about solving the problems the medium throws up. They might attempt to dramatise well-known stories, or more confident writers will probably want to make up their own. I have heard older Key Stage 2 pupils making spoken, lightly dramatised versions of tales for younger listeners to hear on headphones in their classrooms. The outcomes can be played in a number of settings, and they are simple and cheap to make. They give excellent opportunities for a number of related assessment activities, including the elusive speaking and listening criteria.

Having made sense of radio drama, there are other aspects of the medium worth exploring, including interviewing and talks. Operating a school Radio Station is a challenge which has been taken up by a number of primary schools. Children learn to make programmes which have to meet the needs and interests of their audiences; they learn to relate and balance different sorts of programme and they also have real opportunities to work under pressure in real-life situations, make collaborative decisions and gain enormous pleasure without the prospect of doing any damage if it goes wrong!

Information technology

The relationship between language learning and development and IT has been known by many teachers for a long time, but has often been difficult to explore because of lack of resources or access to equipment. Nevertheless, there is increasing evidence of the use of IT to produce written work, particularly, and word processing programs and desk top publishing systems are being used by children to present work in enhanced ways. Larger numbers of pupils have computers at home and it is not unusual for pupils to bring into school work which has originated from topics begun at home, or has been taken home to complete.

One area to which I wish to give special emphasis in the context of more able language users is that of **authoring programmes**. These devices, usually on CD, allow pupils to make integrated presentations of words, pictures, sound, animation and video (although the last item takes up rather too much computer memory to make it really feasible for many pupils). Multi-media authoring combines all the best challenges of writing tasks, and more. Authors have to make clear decisions about audiences, and then meet their needs through all sorts of considerations about layout, style and legibility. They also have to work out how the 'reader' will move from one screen to another, and the particular details which demand extra information. Because there are so many possible combinations of presentational features, authors have to learn to be self-controlled to achieve the best effects.

Once again, the opportunity to talk about what is to be produced is vital to the whole process.

This facility really does have much to commend itself to able language users. The quality of presentations can be really professional and so much more interesting than straightforward written pieces. The children are not constrained by their own drawing skills, but can call on a whole world of illustrations, to which they can contribute by taking their own pictures. If a school has access to a digital camera, so much the better, but it is not essential. They can use this tool to teach, which is the most effective way to learn, and they have an opportunity to review the way they know how information texts work. It is possible to be too self-indulgent with this device and not produce much at all, which means learning planning and schedule scales, not unlike story boarding, within the pupils' realistic limits. There is no doubt, however, that in a very short space of time all pupils will be working with such devices. Annual competitions, such as the National Education Media Awards, organised by the National Council for Educational Technology have seen the most talented and impressive results from this system from schools in all Key Stages. Encouraging work on this medium would be a real pleasure and challenge for more able pupils to enjoy and exploit.

Appendix: Reading List Models

Text	Comments	Suggested further reading
The Chocolate War *Robert Cormier*	Robert Cormier writes adult novels for teenagers. The novel has big themes – power, corruption, the individual in society – as it tells the story of a gang trying to control an American Public School. The gang of students terrorise the ineffectual staff and anyone who dares to stand up to them. One student decides he cannot accept the gang and does just that. A good study of what motivates a character and of evil. It is interesting to go on to compare this with **Unman, Wittering & Zigo**, a play by *Giles Cooper.*	**Brighton Rock** – *Graham Greene* Set in Brighton in the 1930's, Pinkie, a 17 year old gangster, takes his ambition to the limits until Ida, an older woman, determines to convict him for murder. A beautifully written text, with a horribly evil central character and the best finale line of any novel this century. **I am the Cheese** – Another tense psychological thriller by *Robert Cormier*. In a different, more fragmented and challenging style. **1984** – *George Orwell* Orwell's prophetic vision of the ultimate totalitarian state and one man's attempt to establish his identity within it.
Cider with Rosie *Laurie Lee*	Rites of passage tale of growing up as a young adolescent male in the early 20th Century in Gloucestershire. The author, writing autobiographically, examines social divisions of the time. Poetic, charming and funny.	**Sons & Lovers** – *D H Lawrence* Family loyalties and tensions in a Midlands mining community at the turn of the 20th century. Passages of excellent description. **Portrait of the Artist as a Man** – *James Joyce* Stephen Dedalus grows up in Southern Ireland, at the turn of the century, coming to terms with his family, his sexuality and his own difference from his friends and the Irish people. Beautifully written. **The House of the Spirits** – *Isabel Allende* An extraordinary, free-wheeling, exciting and busy tale of four generations of a South American family.

Sample page from *Reading Well* (Sue Maguire and Geoff Dean)

Read On!

A guide for readers who want to move from teenagers' books towards adult books.

BOOKS FOR THE LADS:-
Anthony Burgess - *Clockwork Orange*
Paul Auster - *Moon Palace*
Cormac McCarthy - *All the Pretty Horses*
Jack Kerouac - *On the Road*

HEROES AND HEROINES
Tess of the D'Urbervilles by Thomas Hardy
Roll of Thunder, hear my cry by Mildred D Taylor
A Tale of Two Cities by Charles Dickens
Jane Eyre by Charlotte Bronte
The Odyssey - any English version
Tales of the Norse Gods and Heroes - any English version

FOR REAL BOOKWORMS & MATURE READERS:
Pride and Prejudice by Jane Austen
Wuthering Heights by Emily Bronte
Silas Marner by George Eliot
The Great Gatsby by F Scott Fitzgerald
A Room with a View by E M Forster
Brighton Rock by Graham Greene
Far From the Madding Crowd by Thomas Hardy
The Go Between by L P Hartley
The Old Man and the Sea by Ernest Hemingway
A High Wind in Jamaica by Richard Hughes
The Virgin and the Gypsy by D H Lawrence
Cry the Beloved Country by Alan Paton
The Catcher in the Rye by J D Salinger
A History of the World in Ten and a Half Chapters by Julian Barnes
Ragtime by E L Doctorow
The French Lieutenant's Woman by John Fowles
A Prayer for Owen Meany by John Irving
The Member of the Wedding by Carson McCullers
Heartstones by Ruth Rendell
Camomile Lawn by Mary Wesley
The Secret History by Donna Tartt
Rebecca by Daphne du Maurier
Oranges are not the only fruit by Jeanette Winterson
The Wasp Factory by Iain Banks
Northanger Abbey by Jane Austen

MYTHS AND FANTASIES
Animal Farm by George Orwell
Dragon Slayer by Rosemary Sutcliffe
Sir Gawain and the Green Knight - any modern English version
Lord of the Flies by William Golding
I'm the King of the Castle by Susan Hill
The Once and Future King by T H White
Taliesin, Merlin, Arthur by Stephen Lawhead (trilogy)

PEOPLE AND ENVIRONMENT
The Village by the Sea by Anita Desai
The Fifth Child by Doris Lessing
I Know why the caged bird sings by Maya Angelou
Roots by Alex Haley
One day in the life of Ivan Denisovitch by Alexander Solzehnitsyn
To Kill a Mockingbird by Harper Lee
Of Mice and Men by John Steinbeck
1984 by George Orwell

This booklist was compiled by the English department of Lord Williams's School, Thame, Oxfordshire.

BIOGRAPHY
Wild Swans by Jung Chang
I Know Why the Caged Bird Sings by Maya Angelou
The Dark Quartet (the Brontes) by Lynne Reid Banks
My Family and Other Animals by Gerald Durrell
A Portrait of the Artist as a Young Man by James Joyce
Cider with Rosie by Laurie Lee

SCHOOL - If you really can't drag yourself away!
Kes by Barry Hines
Gregory's Girl by Bill Forsyth
Come to Mecca by Farukh Dhondy
David Copperfield by Charles Dickens
Cider with Rosie by Laurie Lee
The Prime of Miss Jean Brodie by Muriel Spark

WAR

Empire of the Sun by J G Ballard
Fair Stood the Wind for France by H E Bates
Catch 22 by Joseph Heller
Dispatches by Michael Herr
Hiroshima by John Hersey
All Quiet on the Western Front by Erich Maria Remarque
A Town Like Alice by Neville Shute
Slaughterhouse Five by Kurt Vonnegut
Night by Elie Wiesel

Carrie's War by Nina Bawden
The Diary of Anne Frank by Anne Frank
The Snow Goose by Paul Gallico
Talking in Whispers by James Watson
Brother in the Land by Robert Swindells
Zlata's Diary by Zlata Filipovic

HISTORICAL
I, Claudius by Robert Graves (the Roman *Empire as seen* by the weak, stuttering Emperor Claudius)
Roots by Alex Haley (reconstructed history of a black American Family)
The Chant of Jimmie Blacksmith by Thomas Keneally (conflict between Australian Aborigines and European Settlers)
Fire from Heaven by Mary Renault (Childhood of Alexander the Great)
The Jewel in the Crown by Paul Scott (quartet about the end of the Raj)

SCIENCE FICTION
The Handmaid's Tale by Margaret Attwood
Fahrenheit 451 by Ray Bradbury
Blade Runner by Philip K Dick
Golden Witchbreed by Mary Gentle
Make Room, Make Room by Harry Harrison
Flowers by Algernon by Daniel Keyes
Dune by Frank Herbert
Riddley Walker by Russell Hoban
The Left Hand of Darkness by Ursula LeGuin
Dragonsong by Anne McCaffrey
Franky Furbo by William Wharton

HORROR

Successful writers today include Virginia Andrews, Clive Barker, Ramsay Campbell, Stephen Gallagher, James Herbert, Shaun Hutson, Stephen King (who also writes as Richard Bachman) and Peter Straub.

Classic horror:

Frankenstein by Mary Shelley
Dracula by Bram Stoker

Classic ghost stories:

The Woman in White by Wilkie Collins
The Woman in Black by Susan Hill
The turn of the Screw by Henry James

JUST FOR A LAUGH

The Queen and I by Sue Townsend
Paddy Clarke, Ha,Ha,Ha by Roddy Doyle
Stark by Ben Elton
Lake Wobegon Days by Garrison Keillor
Rumpole of the Bailey by John Mortimer
The Discworld Series by Terry Pratchett
Jeeves and Wooster books by P G Wodehouse
The Long, Dark Teatime of the Soul by Douglas Adams
Mostly Harmless by Douglas Adams
The Darling Buds of May by H E Bates
The Third Policeman by F O'Brian

TRAVEL

In Patagonia by Bruce Chatwin
The Innocent Anthropologist by Nigel Barley
The Lost Continent by Bill Bryson
The Songlines by Bruce Chatwin
Chasing the Monsoon by Alexander Frater
The Great Railway Bazaar by Paul Theroux

AROUND THE WORLD

Most of the books in other sections are by British and North American writers. Here are some books by writers from other parts of the world.

Things fall apart by Chinua Achebe (Nigeria)
My Brilliant Career by Miles Franklin (Australia)
July's People by Nadine Gordimer (South Africa)
Shadows on Our Skin by Jennifer Johnstone (Ireland)
Metamorphosis by Franz Kafka (Czechoslovakia)
One Hundred Years of Solitude by Gabriel Garcia Marquez (Colombia)
Prisoners of War (short stories) by Guy de Maupassant (France)
A Tiger for Malgudi by R K Narayan (India)
Jean de Florette & Manon of the Springs by Marcel Pagnol (France)
One Day in the Life of Ivan Denisovich by Alexander Solzehnitsyn (Russia)

ROMANCE
Light a Penny Candle by Maeve Binchy
Rebecca by Daphne du Maurier
Penmarric by Susan Howatch
The Far Pavillions by M M Kaye
Gone with the Wind by Margaret Mitchell
Doctor Zhivago by Boris Pasternak
The Shell Seekers by Rosamund Pilcher
A Dark and Distant Shore by Reay Tannahill

SPINE CHILLERS
The Woman in Black by Susan Hill
The Mist in the Mirror by Susan Hill
Frankenstein by Mary Shelley
Dracula by Bram Stoker
Ghost Stories by M R James
Tales of Mystery and Imagination Edgar Allan Poe
The Turn of the Screw by Henry James
The Birds (and other stories) by Daphne du Maurier

Some writers: Margery Allingham, Raymond Chandler, Agatha Christie, Colin Dexter, Sir Arthur Conan Doyle, Ruth Rendell, P.D. James, Dick Francis, Colin Forbes

FANTASY
Chronicles of Thomas Covenant (two trilogies) by Stephen Donaldson
The Belgariad and The Mallorean by David Eddings
The Fionavar Tapestry (a trilogy) by Guy Gavriel Kay
Titus Groan, Gormenghast and Titus Alone by Mervyn Peake
The Lord of the Rings by J R Tolkien
Dragonlance Chronicles by Margaret Weiss and Tracy Hickman
There are three very good retellings of the King Arthur legends:
The Mists of Avalon by Marion Zimmer Bradley
The Crystal Cave by Mary Stewart
The Once and Future King by T H White

If you read a book which you
think should be on this list
and isn't please tell your
English teacher

Bibliography

Bain, R., Fitzgerald, B. and Taylor, M. (eds) (1992) *Looking into Language*. London: Hodder and Stoughton.

Cairney, T. (1990) *Teaching Reading Comprehension*. Buckingham: Open University Press.

Chambers, A. (1985) *Booktalk*. Stroud: The Thimble Press.

Chambers, A. (1993) *Tell Me: Children Reading and Talk*. Stroud: The Thimble Press.

Cox, B. (1991) *Cox on Cox*. London: Hodder and Stoughton.

Davies, C. (1996) *What is English Teaching?* Buckingham: Open University Press.

Derewianka, B. (1990) *Exploring How Texts Work*. Newtown NSW: Primary English Teaching Association.

DES (1990) *English in the National Curriculum*. London: HMSO.

DES (1988) *Report of the Committee of Inquiry into the Teaching of English Language* (The Kingman Report). London: HMSO.

DES (1989) *English for Ages 5–16* (The Cox Report). London: HMSO.

DfE (1995) *English in the National Curriculum*. London: HMSO.

Eyre, D. (1997) *Able Children in Ordinary Schools*. London: David Fulton.

Goodwyn, A. (1992) English Teachers and the Cox Models. *English in Education* (NATE) Volume 26, Number 3.

Goodwyn, A. (ed.) (1995) *English and Ability*. London: David Fulton.

Halliday, M. (1978) *Language as Social Semiotic*. London: Arnold.

Hayhoe, M. and Parker, S. (1984) *Working with Fiction*. London: Arnold.

Heath, S. B. (1982) 'What No Bedtime Story Means: Narrative Skills at Home and School', *Language and Society* **11**, 49–76

H.M.I. (1992) *The Education of Very Able Children in Maintained Schools*. London: HMSO.

Kress, G. (1997) *Before Writing*. London: Routledge.

Lewis, M. and Wray, D. (1995) *Developing Children's Non-fiction Writing*. Leamington Spa: Scholastic.

Littlefair, A. (1991) *Reading All Types of Writing*. Buckingham: Open University Press.

Lunzer, E. and Gardner, K. (1979) *The Effective Use of Reading*. London: Heinemann Educational.

Martin, N., D'Arcy, P., Newton, B. and Parker, R. (1976) *Writing and Learning Across the Curriculum* (Schools Council). London: Ward Lock Educational.

Monk, J. 'The Language of Argument in the Writing of Young Children', in Bain, R. *et al.* (eds) (1992) *Looking into Language*. London: Hodder and Stoughton.

Neate, B. (1992) *Finding Out about Finding Out*. London: UKRA, Hodder and Stoughton.

Peim, N. 'Key Stage 4 Back to the Future?', in Protherough, R. and King, P. (eds) (1995) *The Challenge of English in the National Curriculum*. London: Routledge.

Perera, K. (1986) 'Some Linguistic Difficulties in School Textbooks', in Gilham, B. (ed.) (1986) *The Language of School Subjects*. London: Heinemann.

Perera, K. (1992) in *Language in the National Curriculum: Materials for Professional Development*. London: Heinemann.

Phillips, M. (1997) 'Q. Who teaches the teachers? A. People who think that notices telling you not to do things are as important as Shakespeare', in *The Observer* 1.6.97.

Protherough, R. 'English and ability: writing', in Goodwyn, A. (ed.) (1995) *English and Ability*. London: David Fulton.

Protherough, R. and King, P. (eds) (1995) *The Challenge of English in the National Curriculum*. London: Routledge.

Reed, M. (1996) 'Language, Literacy and Learning Across the Curriculum', *Changing English*, **3**, 2 189–200

Reid, D. and Bentley, D. (eds) (1996) *Reading On! Developing Reading at Key Stage 2.* Leamington Spa: Scholastic.

Stainthorp, R. and Hughes, D. (1995) 'Young early readers: a preliminary report of the development of a group of children who were able to read fluently before Key Stage 1', in Raban-Bisby, B., Brooks, G. and Wolfendale, S. (1995) *Developing Language and Literacy*. London: UKRA, Trentham Books.

Styles, M. and Drummond, M.J. (eds) (1993) *The Politics of Reading*. Cambridge: University of Cambridge Institute of Education and Homerton College.

Vygotsky, L., (1986) *Thought and Language*. Cambridge, Mass: Massachusetts Institute of Technology Press.

Watkins, C., Carnell, E., Lodge, C and Whalley, C. (1995) 'Effective Learning' *Research Matters*, **5**. London: Institute of Education.

Webster, A., Beveridge, M. and Reed, M. (1996) *Managing the Literacy Curriculum*. London: Routledge.

Wilkinson, A. (ed.) (1986) *The Writing of Writing*. Milton Keynes: Open University Press.

Wray, D. and Lewis, M. (1997) *Extending Literacy: Children Reading and Writing Non-fiction*. London: Routledge.

Poetry books

Cope, W. (ed.) (1989) *Is That the New Moon? Poems by Women Poets*. London: Lions Teen Tracks.

Moles, T.W. and Moon, A.R. (1963) *An Anthology of Longer Poems*. London: Longmans.

McIntyre, W. R. S. (ed.) (1963) *Vigorous Verse*. London: Macmillan.

Orme, D. (ed.) (1987) *The Windmill Book of Poetry*. London: Heinemann Educational.

Index